Philip Braithwaite

All at Sea in the 1960's

The memoires of a young man who wanted
to see the world and get paid for it

The book was printed
digitally on-demand.

Printed in the European Union on
environmentally friendly, chlorine- and
acid-free paper.

The author is responsible
for the content and correction.

© 2020 united p. c. publisher

ISBN 978-3-7103-4467-1
Cover photo: Philip Braithwaite
Cover design, layout & typesetting:
united p. c. publisher
Internal illustrations: Philip Braithwaite

The images provided by the author have
been printed in the highest possible
quality.

www.united-pc.eu

Contents

About the Author

I was born in Warrington in 1944. I served an electrical engineering apprenticeship with the world renowned, 'Metropolitan Vickers Co Ltd' in Trafford Park. I then served 4 years in the British Merchant Navy, as an Electrical Engineering Officer. travelling mainly to Africa, Australia, the Far East and China.

I then Joined IBM as a computer engineer, in the UK for 12 years, then I went to work and live in South Africa for sixteen years, initially working on mainframe computers, then changing direction completely to the tourist trade in SA. I became a Safari operator, for both wildlife and railways and the photography thereof, these being three of my four passions.

My Fourth passion is steam preservation, both on the rails and the road. In SA I was instrumental in the start up of a road steam preservation group, and a rail preservation group.The latter called 'Reefsteamers' is still active today. In the UK I am currently the owner of a 12 ton live steam road roller and having brought it from SA by container, have fully restored it here and run it to rallies and historic events.

I am married to my wife Helen, and have two sons.
I have co-authored three books with Paul Hurley and have written a number of articles for Old Glory magazine, The Road Roller Association, and the National Traction Engine Trust magazine, and various South African traction magazines.Also articles to The Blue Funnel magazine on maritime issues.

Phil Braithwaite

Acknowledgements

I would like to thank my wife Helen for her patience in proof reading and help in the writing of this book. All photographs have never been published before and are the sole copyright of Phil Braithwaite.

Glossary of Terms

FSA – Full speed away/ahead.
FWE – Finished with engines.
Harry Clough – Rough.
The whole toot – Everything.
Deep Sea voyage – A Voyage crossing one of the world's oceans.
Home Trade – National or European voyage.
ETA – Estimated Time of Arrival.
MV – Motor Vessel.
SS – Steam Ship.
Forward or For'ward – The bows or sharp end on the ship.
Siamese 'fairy' – A lady of the night.
Mega – A hand generated high voltage meter used to ascertain earth leakage problems.
Godown – A Warehouse in Malaysia or Hong Kong.
Sampans – A traditional wooden boat used for the transportation of goods from ship to shore, of Chinese origin but can be seen all over the Far East.
Blues – Full uniform with jacket and full length trousers.
Whites – White shorts and white short sleeved collared shirt with epaulets.
Heave too – To slow down.
Earths on a switch board – Caused by water or dampness or condensation in or on some part of electrical equipment. This must be sorted before any serious damage is done.
A List – Is when the ship is leaning to Port or Starboard, un naturally
R&R – Rest and recreation.
The Channels – The elation and prospects of coming 'home'...

Ode to a Seafarer

'Our lot'

We look to the right,
We look to the left,
We look all around about,
and what do we see?? all around me,
Just sea and sea and sea.
But beneath us all,
is a heart and a soul,
which beats, morning noon and night.
For day upon day we plough our way,
cross oceans of blue and oceans of grey
We work in the heat and the cold and the rain,
And never a once do we complain.
We get frostbitten,sun tanned or just plain canned,
And never a once do we complain
We work hard and play hard,
and are at our best when we cannot rest,
For the sea is often rough, so one must be tough.
And brace oneself for jar and jolt
and rolling about.
We batten gear down,
and lash things up.
We clip on lifeline
and keep on workine'

And never a once do we complain.
To eat one's food is often a test,
but one can only do ones best.
To keep it down let alone digest
But this we all accept
And never a once do we complain.
But the best sight of all and a tonic too,
is the sight of old England,
on yon starboard bow
And way in the distance, a dull bell tolls,
and you know the bar is nigh,
and your spirits they are so high
That you laugh and you cheer and you cry,
Good old England again,
But never a once did we e'r complain.

Phil Braithwaite ... R848947.

1

Introduction

The date is Thursday 20th April 1967... Not the best day in the job that I was involved in at the time, so, leaving early afternoon, on the way home, I thought, I am going to change this situation.

In those days the 'Yellow Pages' was the reference book and the telephone, the communications media. Perusing the pages titled 'Shipping companies', my finger alighted on 'Alfred Holts 'of Liverpool, and I duly noted the Telephone number, of the head office in 'India Buildings'

I was already a qualified Electrical Engineer, having served a five year apprenticeship at the then world renowned 'Metropolitan Vickers Electrical Engineering Company Ltd' in Trafford Park, Manchester. This pointed me to a sea- going engineering position.

On phoning Alfred Holts, India Buildings, my call was forwarded immediately to a man that I was to get to know and respect tremendously. The Electrical Superintendent, Jimmy Quinn.
He asked me all the relevant details, and simply said " Be in my office at 0930hrs tomorrow morning, (Friday 21st April 1967), and we will talk".

By 0900hrs Friday morning, I was entering the beautiful old 'India Buildings', in good time for my appointment with the Electrical Superintendent., Mr Jimmy Quinn.
He wasted no time in sizing me up, explaining the role, the company and its policies.

Being a man of few words, he said " We need young men like you, when can you start?"...

It was the shortest interview that I had ever had. " Monday morning " I said. " Good, be here at 0930hrs, with enough gear for a week" he said. And with that he shook my hand and said "Welcome, look after me and my company needs and I will look after you, all your paperwork and documents will be ready for you by Monday morning." And with that he showed me the door and turned on his heel to continue his daily work.

Like I said, 'A man of few words'...

During the drive home my mind was racing, everything was happening so fast. now I have to resign from my present job, as yet I have told nobody what I am about to do, how would they react, does it matter?

I needn't have worried, my mother was not too happy but dad said 'best thing you could ever do, lad'. And so it was after a weekend preparing for the coming week, that 'My sails were set and the wind was about to blow'...

Monday morning came and I made sure that I was in good time for my meeting at India buildings...first the mug shots, then the medical and then the injections against Cholera and Small-pox. then the discharge book and seaman's card. All done...Contracts were drawn up and presented and duly signed. I was now a company man.

The following morning at 0800hrs found me aboard the MV Elpenor, in N.W.Vittoria dock Birkenhead. She was a single screwed ship with a service speed of 17 knots.

As I was unable to stay on board due to shortage of cabins, I made the journey home each night, a distance of 33 miles, I didn't mind as all my expenses were paid.

My hours were 0800hrs to 1700hrs with tea breaks and an hour for lunch which I had on board, courtesy of a meal ticket.

The relieving Senior Electrician was Kevin Orrel, a young chap of 26 from Blackburn, The Chinese Electrician was Loo Wei Kang, from Hong Kong.

On Tuesday 4th May 1967, at about 1200hrs I joined the SS Ixion, in North Canada Dock Liverpool. She was a single screwed steam turbine driven ship of 10,125tons, built in 1951.

She was used primarily on the run to Australia, and used to carry up to 30 passengers, (supernumeraries), however she no longer carried passengers, but did carry and train cadets, both deck and engineering.

I had been sent to relieve the deep sea junior electrician, John Wightman, for the coasting voyage to Glasgow, however John stayed on board that night, so the senior electrician and myself went home for the night and returned the next day.

The senior electrician was Burt Tilford of Childwall, Liverpool.

Other engineers that I met were;

7th Engineer – Gordon Curtis of Bristol

Fridge man – George Anderson of Kirkaldy the 3rd/4th/and 6th engineers.

As an aside, the previous night an Indian ship had side- swiped the Ixion midships. No serious damage, just scraped the paint off, but that necessitated a paint job whilst in Glasgow.

By 0800hrs the following day I was fully ensconced in my cabin aboard SS Ixion, ready for my first voyage up the Irish sea to Scotland.

The remainder of the day was utilised in finding my way around, taking on board the hand over from the previous electrician, and understanding my subsequent roll in this, my first coastal voyage.

I also arranged for Helen, my girlfriend, to come on board, for dinner, on the Saturday to give her an idea what I would be doing and explaining my roll, as Junior Electrician, on a British Merchant ship. We had to arrange for a formal permit to allow civilians to come aboard.

SS Ixion, seen here in The North Canada Dock Liverpool, on 4th May 1967.
Affectionately known as "9 to one" the Ixion was built at Harland and Wolfe
in Belfast in 1951, and went for scrap in Barcelona on the 12th March 1972.

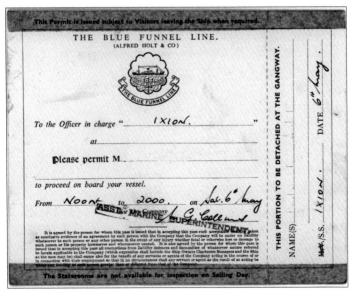

This Permit is issued subject to Visitors leaving the Ship when required.

THE BLUE FUNNEL LINE.
(ALFRED HOLT & CO)

THE BLUE FUNNEL LINE

To the Officer in charge " _____ IXION _____ "

at _____

Please permit M_____

to proceed on board your vessel.

From _____ NOON _____ to _____ 2000 _____ on _____ Sat. 6th May

ASST. MARINE SUPERINTENDENT

for Company

It is agreed by the person for whom this pass is issued that in accepting this pass such acceptance taken as conclusive evidence of an agreement by such person with the Company that the Company will be under no liability whatsoever to such person or any other person in the event of any injury whether fatal or otherwise loss or damage to such person or his property howsoever and wheresoever caused. It is also agreed by the person for whom this pass is issued that in accepting this pass all exemptions from liability defences and immunities of whatsoever nature referred to herein applicable to the Company (which expression shall include the Ship Owners Charterers Managers and the Ship as the case may be) shall enure also for the benefit of any servants or agents of the Company acting in the course of or in connection with their employment so that in no circumstances shall any servant or agent as the result of so acting be under any liability to such person greater than or different from that of the Company.

The Staterooms are not available for inspection on Sailing Day.

THIS PORTION TO BE DETACHED AT THE GANGWAY.

NAME(S) _____

MR /S.S. IXION.

DATE 6th May.

This was a permit to allow civilians on board

Monday the 8th May was my first real working day on board this ship, nothing too difficult, but enough to complete the day. It was known as 'Scheduled Maintenance'.

Tuesday 9th May after some routine duties, down the engine room spaces, the 5th engineer and myself changed into civvies and went to the Birkenhead Mercantile Marine Offices to 'Sign Articles'. This was done by all seagoing staff before any voyage, whether it be a' 'Coasting voyage' or a 'Deep Sea' voyage. Officially known as 'Home Trade' or 'Foreign Trade'.

Thursday 11th May, we were due to sail at 1200hrs, but because of cargo handling delays the ship eventually sailed at 2400hrs, and with a 'standby' from 2330hrs, until we crossed the Mersey bar, to 0300hrs, not much sleep was had that night.

Breakfast was 0730hrs and work was started at 0800hrs.

As per normal the Irish Sea was a bit choppy but by the time we reached the entrance to the River Clyde the sea was like a millpond, and docking in Glasgow was at 1600hrs.

Only one incident was recorded during the short voyage, whilst isolating an earth leakage problem, the supply to the steering gear was tripped for a couple of minutes, causing much mutterings from the bridge.

By Thursday 18th May, at 0400hrs, all cargo had been discharged and the ship was ready to move from Plantation Quay, Princess Dock to Elderslie dry dock, for a repaint, attention to the propeller, shaft and steering gear.

During this time my senior, Bert and myself were engaged in planned maintenance, Planned maintenance ensured that all electrical equipment, fans/motors/winches/generators, etc were overhauled over a 12 month period, ensuring the minimum breakdown, during sea time.

However it was not all work, and Saturday night would see us out on the town. Four of us would go to 'Burn's Cottage', we usually met some young ladies and moved on to 'The Quaich' for a few more drinks. By this time we had usually decided which young lady was for whom, I seem to remember a lovely girl by the name of Jean, that I took a shine too.

Then we would move on down Argyle street to 'Barrowlands', what looked like a converted warehouse where we would dance the night away... After which we would take a taxi back the ship, and fall asleep for what was left of the night... Well we were all young in those days.

Work was the order of the day for the next few days and by Tuesday evening 2100hrs SS Ixion, left KG5 and was 'Full away' by 0100hrs and in the Irish sea bound for Liverpool.

The tide was full by the time we reached Liverpool and the ship docked in Gladstone Dock 'Finished with engines' by 1145 hrs Wednesday 24th May.

SS Ixion is seen here in Gladstone Dock Liverpool after a 'dry docking' in Glasgow in May 1967

Jimmy Quinn (The then Electrical Superintendant) sent another J' Electrician, Bill Fipond down to the SS Ixion, and later the Senior Electrician, Alan Todda also arrived, so that left me spare. So whilst awaiting further orders, what else was there to do but to join in with the engineers for a cabin party with a few beers.

Next day I phoned Jimmy Quinn, and was told to take an extended weekend, and report to him on Tuesday 30th May, and if the MV Maron docked in North West Canada dock to report on board said vessel. However the Maron was only due the next day, so again went home and returned the following day. As you can see one had to be flexible.

By the 31st May, on board the MV Maron I was greeted by the deep sea Senior Electrician Errol Henley Smith, who was handing over to the Coasting/Stand by Senior Electrician Dennis Moles, with whom I was to get to know quite well.

The MV Maron, built 1959, was spotless and more modern than the SS Ixion, however the food was not as good. The Maron was partially computerised, in that it had a mezzanine deck in the engine room right above an auxiliary, V16 Diesel engine, where there were data loggers and electronic equipment, for remote control and monitoring of the ships systems.

In theory these were great and very useful, when they were not being vibrated to pieces by this noisy, vibrating diesel engine.

So on a beautiful sunny evening the ship was moved, by tugs, (Cedergarth, Rosegarth and Maplegarth) from North west Canada dock to Gladstone dock to discharge Latex.

The ship was berthed in South West 2 Gladstone dock, next to the 'RMS Empress of England'. a white passenger ship from the Canadian Pacific Steamship line.

By Saturday 3rd June 1700hrs, Latex discharging being complete, the Maron was moved back to North West Canada dock, by tugs, Cedergarth, Maplegarth and Grassgarth.

RMS (Royal Mail Ship) Empress of England seen here in Gladstone Dock in June 1967, built by Vickers Armstrong of Newcastle and launched in 1956, for Canadian Pacific. She was sold on to Shaw Saville in 1970 and was renamed Ocean Monarch before being scrapped in 1975.

The MV Maron seen here in North West Canada Dock Liverpool in June 1967. Built by The Caledon Shipbuilding and Engineering Co of Dundee in 1960, she was the last 'M' boat to be build and incorporated a data logging system, in the engine room, linked to the engineers accommodation. A for runner to unmanned engine rooms.In 1975 she was renamed Rhexenor and in 1977 to Elder Dempster, as the Opobo. Sold in 1978 and renamed Elfortune, under a Cyprus flag, before being sold on to Greece, as Europe 11. From 1982 she seems to have been laid up until being scrapped in 1987 in Aliaga in Turkey

Sunday 4th June was a quiet day on board, only 4 of us on duty, that day, they call it 'Standing bye'. It was strange really only the hum of the generators, the screeching of the seagulls, fighting over scraps and the occasional curse issuing from the galley as the chef drops something. The dock sides were also quiet, no cargo being worked.

However this would soon all change, as by Monday morning, the hordes of dockers, dock side workers and ships staff would appear and the noise level would be multiplied 100 fold.

The engineers have been doing major repair work on the main engine in readiness for sailing to Glasgow during the week.

One did however have the evenings off, so the cinemas were visited. Monday evening 'The night of the Generals' at the 'Scala' Tuesday evening 'Funeral in Berlin' at the 'Majestic', both in Liverpool. Well you had to do something, with your time, and it was good sometimes to get off the ship for a while.

After the main engines had been reassembled, engines trials were conducted, in the dock, various problems were ironed out and the ship was passed for sea worthiness and the short voyage to Glasgow would be on schedule, after we had had boat drill and inspection.

By 2000hrs we had 'cast off' and were 'full away' by 2200hrs. I watched the last glimmer of daylight set over the Irish sea, by 2235hrs, before turning in for the night.

Stand bye was rung for the Clyde at 0800hrs, it was a beautiful morning and I was able to spend some time on the promenade deck, to photograph the new QE2 in the later stages of commissioning in John Browns shipyard. What a magnificent ship she was.

The MV Maron was scheduled for dry docking in Elderslie, for a full inspection of the hull after a grounding on the previous voyage.

*The Iconic Cunard liner The QE2 at John Browns shipyard on the River
Clyde, Glasgow, June 1967. Her service life was from 1969 to 2008, when
she did the Trans Atlantic crossings and world cruises, until she was retired
as a hotel ship and docked in Dubai, where she still languishes to date*

The MV Maron in Elderslie Dry Dock Glasgow in June 1967

After this inspection and maintenance and a full paint job, we were moved by tugs to KG5 and subsequently cast off and sail back to Liverpool on Friday 6th June. It was a beautiful summers evening with a calm sea. The ship docked in Birkenhead and started loading cargo for her next deep sea voyage. I signed off and was told to take two weeks leave.

On my return I found a telegram waiting for me to report for my first deep sea voyage on the MV Glenearn, from London, wow, this was what I had been waiting for, to see the world.

2

My first deep sea voyage (63) on board MV Glenearn under the AH flag 1967 (Glen and Shire lines)

I had done a number of coastal voyages and many standbys' since joining Blue Funnel in April 1967 as a Junior Electrician, and whilst taking some leave, on arrival at home I found a telegram announcing that I was to join the 'MV Glenearn' in London, the next day. My first deep-sea trip!!!

This is the story of a 23 year old who had never been out of the UK in his life...

10th July 1967 Monday

After a very hurried packing of bags, I managed to catch the 1005hrs bus to Warrington, and after calling at the bank to collect some sterling, caught the
1050hrs train to Liverpool.

At Lime Street Station I left my bags in the left luggage lockers, and went over to Odyssey works to see Jimmy Quinn, my 'super'.

I had my lunch aboard the MV Adrastus, then left for Lime Street Station with my travel warrants.

After collecting my ticket and reclaiming my baggage, I caught the 1430hrs train to London Euston. I then went via the Northern line underground to Kings Cross, then by the Metropolitan Line to Plaistow. There I caught the no. 69 bus to Silverton station and walked from there to the MV Glenearn, in berth 13 of KG5 dock, arriving at 1930hrs... a very long walk with all ones 'gear'.

I very quickly learnt that it was much easier to 'take a taxi'!!!

The Glenearn was a twin screwed vessel of 9100 tons with a service speed of 17knots Powered by two Burmeister and Wain six-legger double acting two stroke engines.

Built in 1938, she had a colourful war record,* and was due for scrap in 1970.

*See "In Time of War" by Alex Aiken ISBN 0 9502134 4 6

The MV Glenearn seen here in KG5 Dock London, in July 1967.
The ship was built at The Caledon Shipbuilding and Engineering Co Ltd of Dundee in 1938. She was a twin screwed ship with two B/W engines. She had a colourful War history as HMS Genearn, and after being returned to the merchant fleet of A/H after the war, was due for scrapping in 1970

The deep-sea senior electrician was Bill Hendrie, and the captain was Greg. J. Wright.

The first night I slept in the cadet's cabin until my cabin was available.

The voyage was scheduled for four and a half months, and because of the Suez Canal crisis we were routed around the 'Cape'.

Tuesday, 11th July 1967

I gradually found my way around the ship and settled in to the Junior Electrician's cabin. This was the ex 2nd Engineer's cabin and was quite spacious. The senior officers moving up to the prom deck and into the passenger accommodation brought this about, now that very few passengers were taken on board.

The evening was spent ashore at 'Anchor House', the mission to seaman in London.

It was a really decent place, plenty of girls, good amenities and a dance most nights, ensuring that any young guy would have a good time.

We were due to sail on the 12th at 1600hrs, but this was delayed due to a port main engine problem! Two injectors needed to be changed as well as a lubricator drive rod.

We eventually moved off from berth 13 of KG 5 just after 1530hrs on the 14th. It was a glorious summers day when we edged into the Thames, and up the estuary, first port of call Las Palmas, Canary Isles.

Saturday, 15th July 1967

Now that we were in the Channel the weather was muggy and still and fraught with banks of sea mist which came and went, necessitating 'slow ahead' for some time, with a 'blow' on the hooter, every two minutes. The P&O liner Cathay caught up with us after leaving London well after we did, and passed us, until she hit the mist bank and slowed and we then caught up. This went on all afternoon, until we were out of the channel and into the Atlantic.

The Bay of Biscay was crossed in glorious sunshine and a slow gradual swell, which as a new boy took a while to get used to.

Along with that are the noises of the wind and waves and the ships vibration, smells and routines. Then the clocks being put back by an hour.

Monday, 17th July 1967

Today was my first working day at sea, starting at 0600hrs and finishing at 1600hrs, a routine that I was to get used to, along with any standbys and/or breakdowns.

After living in the UK, and only knowing the sea to be grey, awaking to see such a pure blue sea and warm wind and blue skies was wonderful.

Just heard that we were due in Las Palmas 0700hrs Wednesday 19th July, for bunkers, then non-stop Penang.

Wednesday, 19th July 1967

Today we changed into 'whites', heavenly cool in the warm climate; also the swimming pool was erected. All the cabins, saloon and dining rooms were decorated in cool eastern materials, and the whole ship took on a new appearance.

We did dock almost on schedule, at 0730hrs in Las Palmas, and proceeded to take on fuel oil.

Las Palmas oozed affluence, although I was not destined to see too much of it, as we had work to do on the Radar scanner. It's gears had stripped and we had to replace the gearbox components, whilst in port and on a stable playing field.

That done it was too late to go ashore, so I watched the Spanish traders trying to sell their wares- all too expensive, I thought.

The doctor needed to come on board to remove a stubborn metal splinter from the leg of the 'Fridge man', and interestingly this doctor arrived in a fawn 1967 Rolls Royce, driven by a lady chauffeur- such was the affluence.

Next the police arrived and gave the 'Hawkers' a ticket, as they were not supposed to sell their wares on the dockside. Something else that was also new to me was that the police all wore guns.

On the forward deck of the MV Glenearn, in Las Palmas,
Canary Isles a vendor displays his wares. July 1967

We sailed from Las Palmas at 1500hrs, weather was clear and sunny and calm.

We were scheduled to arrive in Penang in 25 days time. That night the clocks went back half an hour.

Friday, 21ˢᵗ July 1967

By this date the clocks had been put back another half an hour and the heat of the tropics was building. The swimming pool was very popular. Today between the Tropic of Cancer and the Equator we had our first 'boat and fire drill', commonly known as 'sports day', and I soon saw why.

My job was to assist with the lowering of the lifeboats for boat drill, and to start the emergency generator and to stand-by the emergency switchboard for the fire drill...

Now at sea, my normal working week was Monday to Friday, therefore Saturday and Sunday were my time, so a leisurely day was had, playing table tennis, reading and having a few drinks in the evening.

Heading South in the Atlantic Ocean,
The Glenearn makes steady progress July 1967

However when I awoke that particular morning it was blowing a gale and the ship was moving well, although it was still very clammy. The following day we crossed the equator, at 0200hrs
We sighted our first whale, and she was spouting well.

Monday 24ᵗʰ July1967

After crossing the equator during the night, I awoke at 0530hrs, to start my working day, to a calm sea with a thick fog, an orange fog, which changed to a yellow fog, and then blue grey, before the sun finally broke through and dispersed it unceremoniously.

From the stream of whale sperm all around us, it appeared that we were in the wake of a school of whales.

In the afternoon we had the ceremony of crossing the equator, in which the King Neptune and the Queen (In this case the 3ʳᵈ and Chief engineers), presided over a court, in which the Master was the judge.

Crossing the line ceremony The court of King Neptune presides and gives sentence. MV Glenearn July 1967

The ceremony consisted of capturing, one by one, all those who hadn't crossed the line before and bringing them before the court, to answer the accusation of 'crossing the line without the permission of the King'.

Each was painted with flour, water and anything handy, and made to swallow a pill of icing sugar and salt. (When I say a pill it was the size of a golf ball). After pleading 'guilty or not guilty', it made no difference, each of us were made to 'walk the plank', (of the swimming pool) assisted where necessary, and ducked 3 times.

On this occasion there were 8 of us convicted and made to walk the plank, we were 7th, 6th, 5th engineers, Senior and junior elecs, 2 cadets and the 1st mate.

As compensation, we did, in due course, receive our certificates to say that we had been initiated and given permission to cross the line whenever we so wanted.

The following day the weather was rough, with gale force winds and white horses on the tops of the waves. The clocks were still going forward, by ¾ of an hour, and ½ an hour per night.

We were now in the Southern hemisphere and as we approached the Cape, the weather deteriorated even more, with grey skies and a cold wind blowing an unholy gale. As we cut through it spray was sent high over the bridge and rigging, whistling then howling. The ship, still doing about 17knots, bucked and rolled incessantly.

It was now raining hard, and made every day jobs almost impossible, even writing this was difficult, eating was restricted to sandwiches.

I watched a tanker as it passed us on its way north, ploughing through the waves, disappearing and reappearing miraculously.

We were due to pass the Cape at 1600hrs 30th July 1967, be in the Indian Ocean by 2000hrs, and be again heading North by the next day. Land could not have been too far away, as seagulls and seals appeared. Again the clocks went forward by ½ an hour.

The next morning the weather was no better, with waves of fifteen to twenty feet, but with a tail wind we were making good time, even though the engine revs were reduced. With the props out of the water the revs would rise to 110-120 and when she sat back down the revs would be 80-90, thus preventing over- revving.

Going southbound was a 'Mearsk' tanker in its blue livery, fighting its way, the ship at times was completely immersed from stem to stern, only to rise again and dip again.

A truly amazing sight to watch.

Again the clocks went forward ½ an hour, then another ½ an hour.

By now we are all beginning to feel the weariness of fighting the ships movement and the change in one's body clock as we lose time each day.

Thursday, 3rd August 1967

Today was not a good day at sea, still blowing a gale, but warmer, but we had a main engine breakdown, which had to be repaired 'on the run' and then we had to fix the radar, which had also broken down, then the Radio Officer said could we help him diagnose a radio fault, whereby we could only receive, but not transmit messages. After we had sorted this out we were all feeling the worse for wear, and sleep soon descended upon us.

By Monday 7th August 1967 the clocks had advanced some 1 ½ more hours, and although warmer, it was still blowing a gale. By Thursday 10th August 1967 the clocks had advanced some 51/2 hours ahead of GMT, and the sea had eased and the sun was shining. It was during dusk that the MV Meneleus passed us homeward bound, and with the sound of ships hooters, we wished them bon voyage, and gave them due warning of the bad weather they were about to come up against.

Today Saturday, 12th August 1967 loomed hot and sticky. We were due to enter the Straits of Malacca at noon and the Island of Penang some 24 hours later.

Sunday, 13th August 1967

On arrival at Penang Island at 1000hrs and after completion of the customs formalities, we went ashore for the first time in 24days and 19hrs.We also received our first mail from home, and were able to send mail via the agents.

Penang Island by Tri-Shaw, the best way to travel in the hot Malaysian sunshine, August 1967

It was steamy hot, but the rickshaw ride and air-conditioned 'Hong Kong Bar' soon cooled us a bit. We met an American GI, who seemed to have money to burn and insisted on buying us beer, so naturally we didn't refuse, that would have been rude.

He said that he was on R&R from Vietnam, and seemed quite an amiable chap.

The seawater around Penang is a pastel green, probably due to the plankton, and vegetation. Penang seemed quite a large Island, and to me in the 1960's seemed to have a very 'British' influence, driving on the left and typically British road signs and clean white painted buildings.

The beautifully clean building of Penang island, August 1967

There were many temples in Penang, but by now the beer was taking effect, and apart from noticing the beautiful Eastern Asian girls, with their high cheekbones and jet-black hair. By now our shore time was running out and we instructed a rickshaw boy to get us back to the ship by1800hrs. I remember paying him the sum of one dollar, about 2s6d in old UK money.

On my arrival at the Glenearn I told my 'senior elec'., Bill, that I was OK and that he could go ashore. I had some dinner and fell asleep in my cabin.

After some four hours or so I was called out to a winch failure. By the time that was sorted it was dawn and I watched and photographed the sunrise.

By 1000hrs on the 14th August 1967 we had departed Penang and were heading south along the Malacca Straits to Port Swettenham. The Straits were dotted with wooded islands, many looking totally uninhabited.

Arrival at Port Swettenham was on Tuesday at 2330hrs, where we waited at anchor for a berth, which we were allotted at 0600hrs, on Wednesday, 16th August. We then moved alongside the new jetty. Just forward of us was the Nestor. By 1800hrs the same day we were due to depart, the Nestor had already departed and the Adrastus was inching in to the berth ahead of us. We didn't manage any shore leave as we were fixing a winch breakdown.

During standby from Port Swettenham, the SS Ixion was spotted northbound in the Malacca straits. We were due in Singapore 1000hrs 17th August 1967.

We anchored outside the harbour at 0600hrs to take on board some explosives cargo, before proceeding to dock alongside at 1000hrs.

Penang dockside scene with one of our competitors the Ben Line, with the brand new ship Benabanachon her maiden voyage in August 1967.
Built and launched in April 1967 by Charles Connell and Co of Scotstoun Glasgow she was a single screwed Motor Vessel with a top speed of 21 knots. After various changes of ownership it was scrapped in 1988 in Alang by Chaudry Industries

Because of the monsoon rain, cargo handling was delayed and we departed some 24hrs late on the 21st August 1967, en route for Bangkok.

Whilst in Singapore company ships noted were Glenlyon, Nestor, Adrastus, and the Tantelus. After a scorching sunny day we arrived in the Gulf of Thailand at 2030hrs and anchored awaiting a berth. We eventually moved up river but were docked some 10 miles from the city of Bangkok, and to me it seemed in the middle of the jungle.

A launch was provided to take us up to Bangkok, should the need arise. Cargo was worked and we stayed on board.

The heat was intense and we were all glad to get back to sea again for some fresh sea air.

We departed for Singapore at 1530hrs on Sunday 27th August 1967, arrival due 2000hrs the next day. Our arrival was in a monsoon thunderstorm, and we worked late to remove and ship ashore the starboard fridge fan for serious repair in the PSA workshops.

Tuesday, 29th August 1967

I was fortunate enough to go ashore at 0900hrs to sample the shopping delights and bargains of Singapore. This was when I bought my first Sony car radio system. (I Still have this radio today).

Some of the colourful wagons that supplied the markets of Singapore in August 1967

After working for many hours on another fridge fan failure, we set sail for Shanghai at 1415hrs, full away by 1500hrs and then sleep.

Company ships in Singapore were; Diomed, Myrmidan and the Cardiganshire.

Thursday, 7th September 1967

Arrival in the Yangtse river basin was approximately 2000hrs the previous night.

There were millions of huge dragonflies and small birds flying around the ship.

It was expected that we were to anchor here for some time, how long, we did not know.

The weather was steaming hot from 0700hrs to 1900hrs, with temperatures of 95degF in the shade and 115DegF in the sun with a sea temperature of 87degF. The paintwork was too hot to touch and the corking between the deck planking was melting.

Yesterday we were 'honoured' by the very close examination and presence of an American spotter plane, which came very low and then circled us, checking our registration.

Saturday, 9th September 1967

In the morning we were able to move up the Yangtse River and anchored outside the entrance to the Huang Pu River. Shanghai was some 10 miles up this river, but again we were held at anchor, not knowing when we would be moving up river. That evening saw us suffer a tropical rainstorm followed by a typhoon warning.

By Monday, 11th September 1967 whilst at anchor, the typhoon hit us with a tremendous force. Fortunately being some way up the river it took some of the sting out of it, but the winds were very strong (off the Gobi desert) and bitterly cold.

After being held at anchor for so long, standby was eventually rung for 0400hrs on Wednesday, 13th September 1967. With the pilot on board, we moved slowly and cautiously up the Huang Pu River, arriving at our designated berth at 0615hrs, just as the sun was breaking through the morning mist.

What a pity that we were not allowed to take photographs, (banned at the time by the authorities), as the sights were amazing.

The river was packed with Junks and Lighters, small craft and many Navy vessels such as chinese destroyers, landing craft, MTB's, all heavily armed, and the guns** were manned and at the ready.

The river 'stunk' although pollution was banned, and all along the quayside were many anti British slogans. The dockers and dock workers, all wearing their blue 'Mao' suits, worked in shifts. One shift would be men and the next would be women, although it was difficult to tell the difference at any time.

Also, all along the dockside, there was a good local loudspeaker system, spouting forth Mao's quotations, and when not doing so playing music of the regime.

We were told that we would be here for some five days, but we knew that that would change.

Steam engines were noted on the quayside shunting around the cargo and their handling gear was very suspect, at times. Very young children were observed working alongside the men and women, so we assumed that school was not an option.

Passing overhead, periodically were Chinese warplanes, presumably on their way to Vietnam? Together with the many warships that go up and down the river.

To bring the Chinese people to work on the docks are large pleasure steamers crammed full, like sardine cans.

After a couple of days of working cargo the 'powers that be' had a meeting, the outcome of which was that we as a ship and ships company were 'blacked', and would probably have to leave by midnight tonight, the 13th September 1967.

It was stated that we were 'blacked' because we had 'dangerous cargo' that we had brought into China, which had been transhipped from the Pembrokeshire, whilst it had been in Hong Kong. Within the last 6 months this was the case for any ship and cargo that had been to Hong Kong.

Now the problem was would they let us out, and if so how long would they keep us at anchor, for pilot changes. Days? weeks? Nobody knew!!

Standby for departure was due to be 0500hrs Thursday, 14th September 1967, It was changed to 0700hrs muster and 0800hrs standby.

To all our surprise we went straight out of the Huang Pu River and down the Yangtse, dropped off the pilot, and headed out to sea at full speed.

After that debacle, we awaited a telegram from London on our next move.

By Friday, 15th September 1967, as ordered by HQ London, we arrived at the anchorage for Tsingtoa at 0830hrs, having changed into 'Blues' as it was now becoming increasingly cold. We moved alongside a day later.

The scenery in Tsingtao was stunning, with rugged mountains and crystal clear waters, with thousands of 'Garfish' a scavenger fish, swimming around the ship.

Tsingtao is a Chinese Naval base and there was much naval activity, and to my surprise, flying boats, taking off and landing. How I wish that I had been allowed to photograph, but alas that would have been more than my life was worth.

There were six armed guards on board to make sure that we did not take photos- a pity really as the bay was covered with Junks and shipping coming and going in and out of the mist, with the streaking sunshine breaking through.

On the quayside, steam engines were shunting the cargo wagons around, but alas we were again blacklisted, so with no cargo worked we were cleared of immigration and customs in record time and ordered to leave. We left at 1700hrs and were 'full away' by 1830hrs; our orders were to proceed to Borneo, down the Rejang River; Still we had no fridge cargo.

On our way down the North China sea, we logged the MV Pysander, en route to Japan, she, being at the time 'brand new'!

It was now becoming warmer and together with changing to 'whites' I decided to shave off my beard, that I had nurtured all voyage.

Arrival at initial anchorage was 0830hrs on Friday 22nd September 1967 at the mouth of the Rajang River, subsequently moving up river at 1345hrs to another anchorage where we could work cargo via Lighters and Barges. To the uninitiated, it was just a jungle, but to the locals it was home.

Cargo was worked day and night until Wednesday 27th September 1967, with much noise and gusto until our departure at 0630hrs, when we sailed out of the river, next stop Singapore. Great to have a breeze through your cabin after being cooked up in the jungle, with the mosquitoes and humidity.

Arrival at 'The roads' was 0930hrs and alongside by 1330hrs on Thursday, 28th September 1967.

Cargo was worked solidly until our departure on Tuesday, 3rd October 1967.

Company ships noted in Singapore were MV Achilles, MV Patroculus, SSTantalus, MV Rhexenor, MV Antilochus and my first sighting of the MV Centaur, in all its pure, white glory- a beautiful ship.

I was fortunate to have some time ashore on the Saturday and Sunday, so I bought lots of gear and did some sight- seeing, taking in the Tiger Balm Gardens and the botanical gardens and taking many photographs of the local people and the shipping.

The way of life for the people of Singapore and how they get around,
from pushbike to sampan

Our departure from Singapore was 1700hrs, due in Port Swettenham in 12 hrs time.

We arrived at Deep Water Point at 0515hrs, and were alongside by 0600hrs on the Thursday, 5th October 1967.

On my first 'sortie' ashore in Port Swettenham, I sampled the delights of the superb mariners club, having a swim in the delightful pool and a drink in the scrupulously clean bar, before walking down through the campons, downtown and on to a recommended restaurant for my first Chinese meal- 'Chinese style'. It was great!!

The evening was rounded off by a visit to the 'Port View Club' for a few beers, and then getting soaked by a monsoon downpour on our way back to the ship.

Saturday, 7th October 1967 dawned, sunny and bright and hot. As I had the day off it was decided to go up the jungle to Kuala Lumpur.

As it was my first time I went by taxi, ($10), and had a good walk around and took many photos. It was a big place and even in the 60's it had many new developments. I was very impressed by the buildings and the general infrastructure, and in particular the railway station building, which was the most impressive and clean and architecturally pleasing railway building that I had ever seen. It was black, white and gold and immaculate, and was on a curve similar to York station UK.

The magnificent Railway Station in Kuala Lumpur, Malaysia The station was built in 1910 to replace the old station, and is notable for its architecture based on Eastern and Western designs, and was painted in white and gold. The steam engine No 564.32 known as the 04 pacific's were built by North British Locomotive Co Ltd, the last being delivered by 1947. They were modern oil burning 3 cylinder engines

To a railway enthusiast, as was one of my interests, it was 'Mecca'.

The gauge was metre gauge, the locomotives were steam but oil fired, and the engines, mainly of the 4-6-2 wheel arrangement, were painted in green or black livery. They were immaculate and named in both English and Malay, with brass and copper adornments. They were built by North British Railway Co in 1948/9.

The coaching stock was 'chocolate and cream' built by Metro Cammell UK. Diesel locomotives were built by EECo. UK or

Osaka, Japan. The people were all well dressed, some brightly coloured. They seemed to be very happy, and appeared to have jobs and transport.

My return to Port Swettenham was by train, just 85cents, a haircut and a few more beers before returning to the ship.

Other company ships in Port Swettenham were MV Anchises, and MV Glenlyon.

We sailed from Port Swettenham at 2000hrs and arrived Penang 0830hrs Monday 9th October 1967, where cargo was loaded in the form of Latex, (deep tanks) tin, timber and rubber.

I went ashore at lunchtime, caught a trishaw and visited the 'Snake Temple', again taking many photographs. We sailed in the early hours, 0315hrs, and next day for Phuket.

With only a short stay here, there was no time to go ashore, but I did manage some good photos of the beautiful islands and scenery and local people and sunset, before sailing at 2300hrs for Colombo Ceylon.

The clocks were retarded some 60minutes and arrival at Colombo was 2130hrs Friday 13th October 1967.

The Rupee was the Ceylonese currency and was then 1Rupee= 1/-(5p). I ventured ashore in the afternoon to the Seaman's Mission, and was told that the only decent place for food was the 'Taprobane Hotel'.

Now, to the uninitiated, and that was me, the poverty and squalor was an eye opener, and the sights and smells pervading the air were obnoxious, but you did get used to it and even though the kids pestered you all the time, it was well worth the effort to experience it all.

The railways had steam engines similar to the British GWR 'pannier' tank engines but on a larger gauge- looked like 5ft 2" +/-. The passenger services were DMUs (diesel multiple units) there were still old steam lorries in the streets. It felt as if you had stepped back 40 years in time.

There was a large zoo (Dehiwala) some 7 miles out of town, on the no132 bus from the Mission (plus locals/cattle and all), which cost 30cents, a couple of mosques and a large Cathedral (RC Santa Lucia) and Mount Lavinia.

Apart from that Colombo appeared to be a rundown town, with a lazy laid-back attitude.

Friday, 20th October 1967 dawned the roughest and wettest that Ceylon had known for many years, the sea was breaking over the breakwater and lighthouse to the height of 100ft and more. The harbour was closed and all shipping movements impossible.

Many ships' ropes and wires snapped, including ours, two after and three forward ropes went and we lost two Lighters, which merrily floated off after their moorings snapped.

Two Company ships were alongside us, the MV Antilochus, and the MV Pysander.

Earlier in the week the SS Myrmidon was beside us.

This was the busy scene that greeted us as we entered the harbour at Colombo Ceylon in October 1967. Many ships from all over the world

Saturday, 21st October 1967, at 2130hrs saw us depart Ceylon and head out to sea across the Indian Ocean- next port of call Durban, South Africa.

By Wednesday, 25th October 1967, and the weather still rough, the clocks had been retarded by some 1 ½ hours- no ships had been sighted.

Although the temperature had dropped the seas were still rough with a strong wind sending waves over us 20 to 30 feet high. Being fully loaded, we wallowed considerably until we were in sight of Madagascar. By the 30th October 1967, the ship was due in Durban by 1300hrs.

On our arrival we anchored, and the agents came on board with the pilot, only to be told by them that it was too rough to attempt any entry into Durban-not to mention that there were sixteen ships awaiting entry before us, and to continue on to East London, 24hrs down the coast, where by that time the weather should have abated.

So after having picked up the mail and sent off the voyage reports, we were full away to East London, having only a distant brief encounter with Durban.

Two of the ships noted were 'Frank Lykes' of the Lykes lines and a Brock ship named 'Maiden'.

By Tuesday, 31st October 1967, we arrived in East London at approximately 1130hrs and were at anchor awaiting a berth for 'bunkers and water'. The scenery was magnificent, with colour and flora, and the water was crystal clear. We sat on the bulwarks and fished with a hook and line, whilst we awaited the pilot.

With the pilot on board we docked about 1730hrs. The dockside areas were all clean, modern, and efficient looking, but to my surprise served with steam locomotives.

Being of German design, 'Krupp', they were hauling coal trains to the dock loading areas. They were clean and painted black and green, and of the 4-8-0 and 4-8-4 wheel arrangements. They had large lamps, forward and aft, and 'cowcatchers'...They had Walsherts valve gear and a triple tone whistle. Braking was auto vacuum control.

Diesels were also in evidence in the form of English Electric BO-BO wheels arrangements, and were mainly seen in dual sets and were painted brown...

From what I saw then, my thoughts were that South Africa would be a great place to live and work.

How that was to come true, many years later, is the subject of another scenario in my life!!!

After bunkering, departure was set at 2130hrs; next stop Las Palmas Canary Islands.

Tuesday, 7th November 1967. The homeward bound journey was good weather- wise with only 'one stop' and 'slow ahead' on one engine, whilst a broken lubricator arm was replaced on the starboard engine.

The 'Perseus' was passed en route, and today 7th; news was passed to us from the Perseus of the 'Lewisham train disaster'.

Clocks were retarded; by now some 1-½ hours, and with the weather holding good Las Palmas was entered at 2000hrs. Again this was only for bunkering and water and the mail. At the time 150 Pesetas = £1-00

We were ready to set sail by 0200hrs, 13th November 1967, and with the pilot on board, the main ropes were cast off, but two of the crew were unaccounted for! The fridge man and the 6EO! The good Captain waited until 0326hrs, when two figures staggered down the dockside, and just made the gangplank as standby was rung and ropes were cast off. My, that was close!!

Needless to say they were up before the chief the next day!!

At a steady 16 ½ knots we were due at the Brixham pilot station at 1900hrs on Thursday, 16th November 1967. Crossing the Bay of Biscay we noted MV Prometheus and the MV Pembrokeshire

The Brixham pilot was picked up at 2030hrs, and our scheduled arrival at Tilbury was 1500hrs on 17th November 1967.

Folkestone and Dover were passed, and we could clearly see the white cliffs, and the 'Channels' had really set in. It was bitterly cold on deck with only moderate to good visibility, and the Dover 'fog horn' was wailing mournfully, but to me on my first 'deep sea', it was home!

The Thames was entered at 1330hrs, and the Gravesend pilot was picked up to take us that last short run to Tilbury. We arrived at the old oiling jetty at Tilbury at 1515hrs, only to be told that the ship had to be off the jetty by 1730hrs, because of the tide. At this stage the national dock strikes were also in full swing, with all its serious repercussions.

We were signed off, cleared by customs, collected our travel warrants and away in no time at all. Six of us caught a minibus to Kings Cross, and Euston railway stations.

My train was the 1905hrs Blackpool Express from London Euston.

After what seemed an eternity, arrival at Warrington was at 2215hrs, and on time.

Because of the late hour I caught a taxi home, arriving about 2300hrs, for a welcome two weeks leave.

For a young guy who had never been out of England before it was the beginnings of an interest in travel, different cultures, many more voyages and a broadening of the mind that only travel can do, and what's more everlasting friendships.

Sights such as this the MV Glenearn birthed alongside
the single terminal in Tricomalee in March 1968, now gone forever,
will recede into the annuls of history

3

My Second Foreign Going voyage (64)
on the MV Glenearn

After my leave I was due back on board the MV Glenearn, Monday 11th December 1967.

To this end, a train was caught, the 1310hrs train from Warrington Bank Quay station, and arrived with my deep sea gear at 1800hrs. The ship was in the same berth in KGV as per the last trip, and the deep sea Senior Electrician was Bill Benson. We were due to sail on Wednesday at 2030hrs, but as yet our destinations were uncertain. This was because of the Suez crisis and whether or not we would be able to go through Suez or have to go around the Cape, A much longer journey.

We did, however,sail on schedule, but encountered bad weather, fog, in the English channel, which caused a very long stand bye, and we weren't 'Full Away' until 1400hrs on the 15th December.

By now I knew the ship inside out, and I settled down to the sea life routine very quickly. As we headed South the sea and air temperatures rose to more pleasant levels.

By our arrival at the Canary Isles, our voyage routes had been confirmed,. It was to be around the Cape, up the Indian ocean to rejoin our normal routine at Penang.

However, a small problem on the Starboard engine slowed us somewhat, and we continued for some six hours on one engine only. We all turned too to help repair the engine, which had sheared an exhaust piston rod. Although an electrical engineer, being a strong young man I always turned out to help the engineers, this I found helped me understand the workings of engines and was to stand me in good stead, for the future.

We were very quickly back to our service speed of 17knots, on twins screws, and by the evening we passed the MV Automedon, homeward bound, with the customary exchange of hooters.

The ship arrived in Las Palmas for bunkers and the mail, most of the time was taken up by further adjustments to the Starboard engine, before we sailed the following morning for Penang, via the Cape.

The equator was crossed on Friday the 22nd at midnight, and the lead up to Christmas was in the South Atlantic. now this was my first Christmas at sea and the first time that I had been away from my family. However the ship took on a very festive feeling, the seas were calm and blue and for the first time I experienced a warm Christmas.

The No 1 steward had made sure the saloon/dining rooms and bars were brightly decorated and cheerful for all to enjoy.

There was a large Christmas cake and mince pies and the Christmas menu was superb.

On Christmas day we were passed by the ship' The Windsor Castle' all lit up and we exchanged Christmas greeting on the RT as well as the hooters.

On the 28th we passed the MV Glengarry homeward bound.

Also I received a ships telegram, which was a lovely Christmas present to receive... See Fig 1.

Also the same day we saw a Killer whale heading South, some 200 miles from Capetown South Africa, which we were due to pass on the 29th in the early morning the weather was still calm and warm...

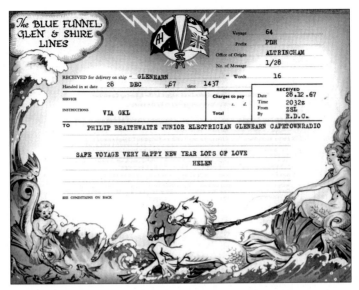

An example of the beautiful old ships telegram that we used to receive

The Glen and Shire house flag

The New year was also suitably brought in and much fun and laughter was had by all.

NEW YEARS DAY DINNER MENU.

MV GLENEARN AT SEA 1968 ...

HAPPY NEW YEAR TO ONE AND ALL.

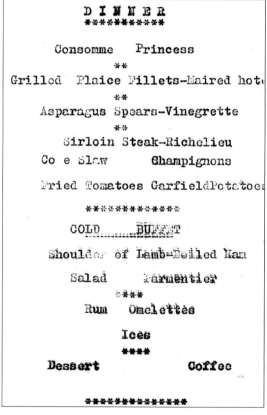

The menu for the New Year's dinner 1968 aboard the MV Glenearn

Capetown was passed on the 29th December and was an amazing spectacle.

It was beautiful weather and porpoises, dolphins and sealions could be seen and photographed. table mountain had the 'tablecloth' draped over it with blue skys and cumulous clouds.

By the evening we were in the Indian ocean and the first waterspout could be seen, whipping the sea up into a vortex, with a whirlpool beneath it, quite spectacular.

By Sunday 31st December we were anchored off Durban, due to go alongside 1700hrs that day.

On New years day 1st January 1968, we collected the mail. Alongside us in Durban was the ex Blue Funnel ship MV Mentor, sold to a Greek shipping company and looking very sad. Depature was 1505hrs heading North past Madagascar, and on Northbound up the Indian ocean to the Island of Penang and Malaysia.

The wind had risen overnight, but by the time we passed Reunion Isle and Mauritious, and headed past the Chagos Archipelogos, it eased, and a large whale was spotted following us. Our expected time of arrival Penang was noon Saturday 13th January.

Before arrival at Penang we witnessed many squalls of rain that emmenated from large cumulous clouds accompanied by full rainbows, sometimes almost a full circle.

Just prior to our arrival in Penang we had a scavenge fire in the port engine, necessitating reduced revs and fighting the fire until it was completely extinguished.

As we did not want to enter port with this scavenge fire, as you should not stop the engine during this process, but maintain a slow ahead until extinguished, we sailed in a circle for some five hours, until extinguished, finally entering the port of Penang, dropping anchor for an hour or so until finally going alongside at 1945hrs.

The oportunity to stretch ones legs was taken for a couple of hours, walking ashore fot the first time in a month. It was very pleasant and clean. Bunkers were taken and standby was due 1100hrs, for an arrival in Port Swettenham at 2300hrs.

Subsequent arrival at deep water point was 2345hrs, and we finally docked and were FWE by 0730hrs on the 15th January 1968.

The next day, we went ashore to the Mariners club for a swim, beautiful pool, good food and ice cold beer.

A Montage of two photos of the beautiful swimming pool at the Mariners club in Port Swettenham Malaysia, in 1968

We were very lucky to have the use of these facilities, which were in most ports of call.

Our stay in any port in those days was totally dependent on cargo, both unloading and loading, and in many instances would take from three to five days. Although some of that time one would be working, a good proportion of the time was yours, to do with it what you wanted.

Our departure from Port Swettenham was in the early hours of the 17th January for an arrival in the Western roads of the Malacca Straits for Singapore, some 24 hours later. However in this instance there were some 22 ships waiting for a berth so we stayed at anchor, and awaited our turn. Some company ships noted were MV Flintshire, and the MV Nestor.

The photo shows the entrance to Singapore docklands.

As one enters the Port of Singapore, the pilot boat precedes us and the 'Welcome' sign greets you

The MV Pyrrhus, docked in Singapore 1968. She was built at Cammell Lairds in Birkenhead in 1949, and after suffering a fire in November 1964, in Gladstone dock Liverpool, and being repaired went on until 1972 when she was sent for scrap to Kaohsiung

After unloading, we departed in the early hours of the 20th January for Bangkok.

Arrival at the anchorage for Bangkok and subsequent move to berth 'shed 9' necessitated a 3 and a half hours stand bye, finally tying up at 1030hrs. A walk ashore that afternoon included a stroll through the local markets, where one could see how the local people lived and what they ate and drank. A swim in the wonderful Mariners club pool cooled you off, followed by a local beer, before returning to the ship for dinner. It was tough being at sea in those days...

*The Temple of the Emerald Buddha and
a local market scene in Bangkok, Thailand*

A boat trip that we organised to see the canal markets of Bangkok

The 'Royal Barge' in full cry in January 1968. From an article on the internet Quote: "The most impressive and important of the boats is Suphanahong, the King's personal barge. Built in 1911 to resemble a mythical swan, the 46 metre craft was hewn from a single tree and is covered with intricate gilt carvings and colourful pieces of glass, forming an eye-catching mosaic. There is a golden pavilion on board to house the King and his Royal family. It is not an easy task to get this vessel moving; it requires 54 oarsmen, who paddle in time to the rhythmic beat of a drummer following a melodic chant called a "bot heh rua.""

The next day a tour had been organised to go up the canal markets and to a Thai silk factory, where the whole process of manufacturing silk was explained, and where one could buy dress lengths for ones wives and girl friends and mothers, at reasonable prices. After some lunch, 'alfresco' of course the Royal Barges were visited. This was in a huge shed, accessed by plank bridges and consisted of a 'Queens' barge, a 'Kings' barge and a number of others for the entourages. Periodically there would be a race between them, providing a right royal spectacle. These boats were very ornamental and were propelled by numerous oarsmen, who rowed to the beat of a drum.

Before returning to the ship a visit to 'The Temple of Dawn' was offered. very interesting, as it was still being built and had already been under construction for the past ten years. And like most temples was very ornate, and covered with gold paint and gold leaf.Beautiful gardens and many individual places of worship, for the resident monks, and the public.

Departure from the wonderful city of Bangkok was on Thursday 25th January 1968, it was hot and humid and oh what a pleasure it was to get a sea breeze through your cabin.

Next port of call was Shanghai, North Communist China.

This entailed sailing South past Laos and Cambodia and Vietnam, said quickly, not that far, however being so near a war zone, your presence drew much attention and we were strafed many times by American jet fighters, and asked our intentions and our registration.

We used to put the largest Union Jack flag we could lay our hands on and strap it to the forward hatches. And even then we were still buzzed many times.

A USA destroyer was also deployed to question our 'raisin detre'...

Eventually the South China Seas were reached and we headed NNE towards North communist China.

As we departed Bangkok the following document was issued to all ship's crew.

Which was a shame, as the sights in and around China we knew would be amazing.

Passage through the Taiwan Straits was slow as a fog came down and standby was rang with subsequent slow ahead and periodically blowing the ships hooter. It turned very cold, very quickly and a force 8 gale blew up and by the following morning we were in 'Blues'

A Notice issued by the Chinese customs officials in Shanghai, prohibiting all photography in China.

Chinese New Year was on 30th January. For which they celebrated by having Chinese food and plenty to drink. The junior engineers and myself were not invited.

We were due at the outer anchorages of the Shanghai basin about midnight on Wednesday 31st January.

There were some 10 other ships also waiting, and we wondered how long it would be before it was our turn. We were there for 3 days. And it was freezing!!!!

Together with high winds and sea spray the decks were beginning to freeze solid and ice was forming, adding extra weight to the superstructure of the ship, and she was already high in the water as she was empty. And so we all 'turned too' to chip ice. What a freezing experience that was, 1 hour on and 1 hour off to warm up.

Saturday 3rd February, saw us at anchor again at the mouth of the Hwang Pu river, awaiting our pilot. En route we saw two sunken ships, one was a Chinese ship, the other of unknown registration,as it had broken its back and was sunk by the stern.

One could only surmise the reasons for these wrecks, as being adverse weather, or poor seamanship. One dare not ask!!

What a pity one was not allowed to photograph these disasters. for posterity and history.

We eventually moved alongside at 1730hrs that Saturday and we doubted that we would secure any cargo. And so it was, we were to depart Midnight Sunday 4th February. The decision was taken to turn off all fridge holds. Our departure,however, was deferred to 0800hrs Monday 5th February, we were not given any reason. Just told that fact.

So a decision was taken to hire a taxi and go to see what they would allow us to see of the beautiful city of Shanghai.

The taxi arrived about 1100hrs, and surprisingly was a British Vauxhall Cresta. Four of us shared the cost, two cadets the 5th engineer and myself. It cost the princely sum of 7JMPs, if my memory serves me correctly about 3 US Dollars.

It was about 5 miles from the ship through the docklands to the main city. The roads were mainly rough and cobbled with rail tracks everywhere.The trains were all steam powered and were of the 2-8-0 wheel arrangement, the signalling was semaphore, of the lower quadrant type. The main transport for the people was push bikes, old trams (similar to the Blackpool trams) and trolleybuses, all painted in Green and yellow, albeit peeling off and dirty.Their power supply coming from overhead wires which would spark, arc and crackle as the trams moved from track to track. All modes of transport were old and greatly in need of a coat of paint.

With the old cobble stone roads and ancient buildings you felt as if you had stepped back 20 years in time, and that was in 1968.

It was freezing cold. The people all looked the same in their 'Moa' suits, men and women alike a sea of 'blue' many of them wore heavy great coats against the weather. The tree lined roads were heavily laden with snow and ice. There were hoardings with illuminated pictures of Chairman Moa, statues of him everywhere, and his little red book. Our taxi picked its way to the

'Shanghai Seaman's Club, and friendship store', the only places we were allowed to visit.

It parked outside the door and immediately crowds of people stopped and stared at us.

We were known as the 'Western Decadent Dogs', and although they never uttered a word you knew what they were thinking, having been brainwashed at the time, by the regime. You saw it in their eyes. On reflection you also saw unhappiness and fear.

The Mission to Seamen had more of the look of an old British railway station, than a Mission to Seamen. It was old and could do with a good clean up. It was reputed to have the longest bar in the world, it was long, and the beer was good, and cheap. 'Shanghai beer'. nice.

上海海员俱乐部国际海员物品供应部

SHANGHAI SEAMEN'S CLUB
COMMODITY SUPPLY DEPARTMENT FOR FOREIGN SEAMEN

The Shanghai Seaman's club logo on their brown paper bags, 1968.
The Seaman's club was a former British Merchant's building,
supporting the longest bar in the world, made of mahogany,
according to the English speaking barman

The friendship Store was fascinating and sold all sorts of 'necessities' for the life of the seaman, and was very cheap, so much so that one could not spend your 'jmps'. so a receipt was given for all purchases, which would have to be produced to the authorities on your departure from China. This was because you were not allowed to take Chinese money out of the country, and you would be issued with a receipt which could be redeemed on your next visit.

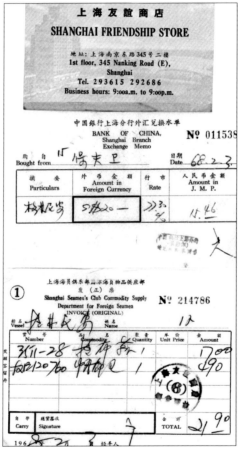

An invoice and a bank of China receipt for goods bought and money exchanged in 1968

We then had the taxi take us back to the ship, as there was a curfew in force. No one on the streets after midnight. However by 2300hrs the city was dead and just like a morgue. Our taxi being the only thing moving.as it rattled its way back to the ship over the uneven cobbles. It was an interesting experience but what photographs one could have taken, had we been allowed.

Muster was 0630hrs for a standby of 0800hrs and the ship sailed for Hong Kong and was FSA by 1200hrs.

By the 6th February, a Tuesday, it was much warmer but the seas were rough and it was raining hard. Ships engines were notched back to avoid over revving when the stern came out of the water, on the rise and fall of the waves.

Arrival at Hong Kong was 1800 hrs, the ship was tied up to the buoys and access to the shore was by tender., to the ferry terminal, or to Holts wharf. or the Star ferry terminal.

A typical view of the ships tied up to the 'Buoys' in Hong Kong in 1968

The Hong Kong ferry to Macau was in 1968 by modern hydrofoil,
this one called 'The Flying Flamingo'

Hong Kong truly lived up to its name 'The Pearl of the Orient'. It was to me the most amazing place in the world, It is abound with Islands and mountains, with mist and cloud swirling around. It has a huge natural harbour, and can accommodate many hundreds of ships, at anchor. The city is like an Oriental New York with its wide tree lined streets and narrow side streets, with neon signs and advertising boards everywhere. At night it is like a fairy land of lights. The local people are well dressed, organised, and seem to be happy.

It is cheap to buy anything, if you are careful and the service is the best that I have ever experienced. The food is excellent, varied, any cuisine, and reasonably priced. Some places keep strict dress codes, like the 'Jockey Club' very formal. The Royal Navy had a base here and the airport, Kai Tak, at the time was fairly small., Although it has subsequently been enlarged, modernised and its runway extended into the harbour.

Kai Tak Airport

*Here we see Kai Tak airport, the lower photograph showing the iconic
De Havilland Comet in 1968*

I was fortunate to have as my good friend and shipmate the
3rd engineer, a Singaporean officer, Billy Yip Cum Tao, to show
me the best places to go in Hong Kong. he also knew a young
lady, an English school teacher (Joan) and she organised another young school teacher, (Nadiya) to accompany us around the
city, and we spent many happy hours site seeing, The Peninsu-
lar Hotel, (One of the 'props' for a James Bond Film). Up the
Peak on the tramway, what a view from the top, the best Chi-

nese restaurants,(The Floating Restaurant) and the best places to shop, without being classed as a tourist. We ventured,in a taxi up the short coast, passed the village of Aberdeen and on up to the Chinese border post, in those days still manned by the army. Looking out over the river of peace to North Communist China, then another world away, paddy fields and more paddy fields. Also beautiful flora and trees.

A Poinsettia, which had grown into a bush shows the beautiful Flora of the region

The Star ferry crossing from Hong Kong to Kowloon

*View of Hong Kong from the 'Peak' at the top
of the funicular Railway in 1968*

There were several Telescopes at the cafe on the top of the peak, and after putting my 50cents in and scanning the horizons and especially the ships in the harbour, I saw a British India ship, called the SS Nowshera. Just another ship, you may say, but my old school friend and fellow engineer was on board the SS Nowshera, coincidence?? He was a Radio Operator. So a plan would have to be made to contact him for a catch up when I returned to the ship.

Other A/H ships in port that day 7th February 1968 were: Peisander, Glenalmond, Antilachus Protesislaus, and the Flintshire.

Plenty of shore time was to be had in Hong Kong and Kowloon, as the ship loaded cargo for some 10 days.

I remember having a light weight suit made by, I think 'Jackie Lee' a recommended tailor. measured in the afternoon, first fitting about 8pm and final fitting and purchase 10am next day, brilliant, what service, with a smile...

One evening was spent with friends at the local cinema, 'The Queens Theatre', on the agenda was James Bond and 'You only live twice'. Unlike British cinemas of the day (1968) this one in Hong Kong was air conditioned, clean and comfortable.

A ticket for 'The Queen's Theatre' to see a 'James Bond' film in 1968

On Sunday 18th February 1968, Standby was rung 1630hrs and we were FSA for the Rajang river, Borneo by1730hrs. Due to anchor at the mouth of the Rajang river at 2030hrs overnight and move up river first light Wednesday 21st February, where the ship dropped anchor at 0830hrs for cargo handling.

It was not the most salubrious of places, and unbearably hot and humid, with mosquitoes like 'Stuka' dive bombers.

Cargo here was logs, logs and more logs. They were in the process of cutting down the rain forests principally to grow palm oil.One never gave it a thought that we too were instrumental in helping to destroy the worlds rain forests.

These logs could be in excess of 12 tons each and used to play havoc with the ships winches and brakes, breakdowns were common so even if I had wanted to any chance of shore leave was unlikely. The logs were floated out to the ship and being wet weighed more that you could imagine.

It was with a sigh of relief that we left The Rajang river at 1500hrs on the 26th February 1968 for Singapore, and drank in the fresh sea breezes. I seem to remember sleeping on deck in a hammock, to keep cool.

On our arrival in Singapore, BF company ships in dock and 'in the roads', on the 28th February 1968 were MV Antilochus, Myrmidon, Glen Almond, Glenfinlas, ...
Also The Passenger Liners Rotterdam and The Iberia...

Cargo was worked, but not very much, as most of our stay was for 'tank cleaning' in readiness for taking on Latex at Port Swettenham. Most of our 'Electrical planned maintenance 'was well in hand giving us much opportunity to 'Go ashore'...
This, one always did, whenever the opportunity presented itself, and so it was that a photographic experience was embarked upon. Armed with plenty of film, an attempt was made to show what Singapore was really like in 1968. here are a few of my endeavours, the docks, the people and the life.

Un loading from the Sampans was always a labour intensive business.
Singapore 1968

Today was a holiday in Singapore, so a walk into town saw the lion dance preceding the go-karting which took place up and down the dual carriageway

Walking on into raffles Square, and capturing the faces of the children and people of Singapore in 1968. One wonders where they are today?

The 'Meter Maid' or 'Parking Warden' of the day

Some more young people of Singapore in 1968

And no visit to Singapore would be complete without a stroll through the world famous 'Tiger Balm Gardens'

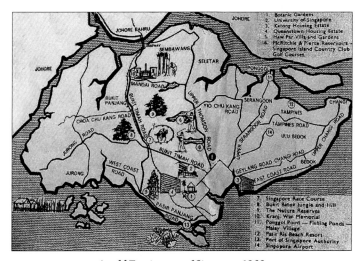

An old Tourist map of Singapore 1968

Raffles Square 1968. Firstly designed by Sir Stamford Raffles as the commercial centre of Singapore in the 1820's it is now home to the tallest skyscrapers in Singapore. But the Raffles Hotel was the original hotel opened in 1887 with 10 rooms for the discerning travellers and commercial merchants and even by 1968 it retained its ambiance as a British Colonial building, with its leather settees and ceiling fans, lofty cool interior spaces and Eastern decor.

And no evening would be complete without an 'Alfresco' meal and a few drinks down 'Bugis Street'

During your return to your ship a sudden monsoon downpour would soak you just getting to your ship. To the left the MV Glenearn, in front of her was the newer MV Glenlyon almost 12,000tons with three quarter midships accommodation, built in Holland in 1962, after various transfers was cut up in 1975 at Kaohsiung

Standby for departure from Singapore was 1530hrs, 3rd March 1968,due in Port Swettenham in the Early hours of the 4th March, it was only a short sailing and revs were reduced to 85 RPM during the night, to make it to the buoys in daylight.

Arrival was 1000hrs at buoy No.1 ... A beautiful still day, albeit hot and humid.

Our cargo here was Latex, which went straight into our heated deep tanks and sealed for the rest of the voyage home.

Tied up at the buoys at Port Swettenham in 1968

At Port Swettenham, cargo was also worked until departure for Penang on the 7th March, this was another short hop and arrival at Penang was 0600hrs on Friday 8th march 1968.

There were only some 24hrs for loading cargo in Penang before our next destination in Ceylon.

Shortly after sailing from Penang, and before the long haul home and as the sea was fairly calm, it was decided to do a full 'boat drill'. So I in my infinite wisdom volunteered, to assist the Radio Officer, along with the other crew.

This entailed lowering a lifeboat with a portable radio on board into the sea, and the ship would then sail over the horizon, and we would make sure communications could be kept loud and clear, and that all on- board systems worked according to The Board of Trade regulations.

Then we would just have to hope that our ship could find us again. It was, indeed an experience ... It is quite amazing how small a boat is in the great expanse of the ocean ...

Arrival at the anchorage, Trincomalee, Ceylon, was in the early hours of the morning, (0100hrs), the 12th March, before moving inside the natural harbour. at 0600hrs.

This natural harbour was stunningly beautiful with lush green vegetation and many islands and beaches. The water was crystal clear and teeming with fish and marine life.

Full bunkers were always taken here before departure as it would be some 22 days before the next stop in the Canary islands.

Cargo was loaded here in Trincomalee from our arrival on Tuesday 12th March to Saturday prior to our departure on Sunday 0630hrs.

Our cargo, Ceylon tea, tea and more tea... In those days in tea chests, by the thousands...

We did however, have some time ashore and were invited to play a game of football, against 'The Trincomalee customs League Team'. And they were good... they won by a resounding 9 to 1. but in our defence it was extremely hot, and they were much fitter than we were, but hey it was fun...

A walk ashore was always interesting. The way of life was slow and most vehicles were old black Morris Minors. Animals roamed the streets along with the sacred cows and cattle and down by the seashore, as if time had passed it by. The fishermen were mending their nets and the kids were having fun. Did they go to school, probably not, but they all looked happy.

*Tea chests by the thousands. A scene whilst loading cargo
at Trincomalee, Ceylon*

Transport was by oxen cart, it was very dry and dusty and one
didn't risk eating any street food, only drinks in sealed bottles,
were consumed, mainly local beer then only after wiping the
top carefully, and drinking from the bottle, That was our ex-
cuse, anyway.

One felt that you had stepped back in time some 40 years
or more...

These boats were hollowed out tree trunks with side planks
sewed on, they had outriggers for stability, and were very sea-
worthy albeit very well used and old. Some of them sported a
full sail and rigging, and I am reliably told travelled long dis-
tances at sea.

A local fisherman mending his nets in Trincomalee Ceylon 1968

The MV Glenearn is seen here tied stern first to the jetty, with two forward anchors dropped for stability in Trincomalee, Ceylon. Cargo is being loaded from lighters and boats of all shapes and sizes

Departure from Trincomalee was 17th march1968, and even though we had full bunkers, it was decided to ration fresh water, for the long haul to Las Palmas, it was a basic rationing, and in our opinion was unnecessary...

As we left the Islands of Malaysia a Liberian tanker was spotted, on fire and aground, it's back was broken. However, after investigation, it was ascertained that there was nobody on board, and that the authorities knew about it and our assistance was not required.

By Sunday 24th March, Mauritius and Reunion Islands were passed and Madagascar was on the Horizon, and with only 4 days to go to Capetown SA, the weather and winds were fair, force 5/6, slight swell,temperature 25c, speed 17knots, but barometer falling...

By the afternoon of Monday 25th march the wind had increased to gale force 9, and the waves were up over our decks, and it was expected to last until Capetown was reached.

Meals were reduced to sandwiches and the table clothes were watered, to stop movement.

Drinks were reduced to cold drinks to avoid hot spillage, and all work on deck was suspended.

By Thursday 28th march, the wind had dropped to a force 2/3, but so had the temperature to 14/15deg.c, and we were back in 'Blues', however with the trade winds behind us we were making 18/19 knots.

Albatrosses and Porpoises followed the ship with Dolphins on the bow wave. Whales were spotted, and nearer Capetown seals and sea lions were also spotted along with all the different types of sea gulls and birds.

Arrival in Capetown was Friday 29th March 1968 at 1200hrs. As we were not stopping in Capetown, because we would have to pay 'Harbour dues', we stayed outside the 3 mile limit, and merely collected the mail.

We were FSA again by 1400hrs only to be slowed by a bank of fog for some 2 hours.

What we saw of Capetown, looked really nice, with the beautiful, mountain ranges and Table Top Mountain, Lions peak etc, all too soon disappeared under a blanket of fog.

Some two days out of Capetown we had a scavenge fire on No. 5 port engine and a cracked liner on No; 4 Port engine. This took some 6hrs to extinguish, and a further day to fix the liner ... This resulted in a huge delay in the schedule and an almost certain late arrival in Las Palmas. The end result was a decrease in our speed and we were running out of fresh water and oil. This was also exacerbated, by the cargo shifting and causing a 4 degrees list to Port, staying so until arrival at Las Palmas at 0315hrs on Tuesday 9th April 1968.

By the time we had reached Las Palmas we had run out of fresh water, had ailing engines, and a 4 degrees list to Port. What a performance, and to boot, no mail at Las Palmas.

Some 24hrs was spent in Las Palmas, in which time full bunkers were taken, the list was corrected and the engines were fixed ...

Expected departure for Genoa Italy was 1130hrs and we were FSA by 1200hrs.

The Rock of Gibraltar was passed at 0800hrs on11th April 1968, and we were passed at speed by a British Destroyer HMS Diana, on its way to Gibraltar. Naturally we had to 'Dip' the Red Duster, and HM S Diana acknowledged by the usual 'Whoop, whoop'.

HMS Diana was a 'D' class destroyer, built in 1947 and launched in 1952, built at Yarrow and Co Ltd dockyard, she was a Daring class destroyer , designed by the Royal Navy was based on the Pacific campaign, including long range and the ability to replenish at sea

Arrival at Genoa was 1530hrs Saturday 13th April 1968. Having never been in Italy before I wanted to go ashore, in the short time that we had there, but had to obtain a pass to go ashore.

The formal pass required to 'go ashore' at Genoa Italy

I couldn't get far in the short time I had but I did photograph some steam trains shunting the docks before beating a hasty retreat as the ships hooter was being blown to let you know of the impending departure.

We were FSA by 1206hrs, next stop England and London...

Gibraltar was again passed in the homeward bound run on Tuesday 16th April, and there were many porpoises and dolphins following us. We sailed quite close in to Gibraltar, and had a good view of it, looked very picturesque.

As we entered the English Channel it became quite cool and we once more were back into blues.

Arrival at Tilbury docks was 1430hrs, and we were all signed off by 1630hrs and I caught the 1930 hrs train to Manchester, caught a taxi and was home by 2330hrs, with all my deep sea gear. My second deep sea voyage was complete...

4

Coastal Voyages and Training

After some three weeks of leave, on Tuesday 18th June 1968, I reported to the office at 1030hrs.and was asked to await further orders from Jimmy Quinn... he was delayed until 1300hrs, at which time he told me to report to the MV Kaduna, an Elder Dempster ship in Glasgow KGV dry dock on 20th June for approximately 2 weeks, and to do this I would be acting 'Senior Electrician.'. The ship was on 'shore side power*' and was having some considerable work done and attention to the hull and the main engines.

* 'Shore side power' – This occurs whenever a ship has work done on its auxiliary engines.

The MV Kaduna, an Elder Dempster line ship, built in 1956, seen here at the Scott Lithgow's dry dock, Greenock on the River Clyde near Glasgow. She was taken over by Ocean Fleets, in the late 1960's and sold on in 1973 to Liberia and renamed Regent Reliance

To that end I caught the 0953hrs Perth train from Warrington Bank Quay station, changed at Carlisle, and arrived at Glasgow Central at 1545hrs, caught a taxi and was on board the MV Kaduna at 1615hrs. I thought it ominous when the Senior Electrician avoided me and couldn't wait to get away very early the next morning.

The ship was a 5500grt vessel, in appalling condition electrically, and the engine room was a disgrace.

The cabin allotted to me was a cadets cabin, without any facilities, not even a washbasin, you had to use communal washing and showering facilities.

Well one had to take these circumstances 'on the chin' and put up with it for a couple of weeks...

The MV Kaduna was due to sail at 1800hrs Monday 8th July, 1968, and thankfully she was ready and with a full complement of crew, released me for other duties.

The standby engineers, including myself, were swiftly off the ship by 1755hrs and away to our hotel for the night, before travelling home the next day.

I only then realised why she was a workout. The 'K' boats did not carry an Electrician, hence being in a cadets cabin...

The next morning I caught the 0825 train home to Warrington and was home by taxi at 1500hrs. On my return home there was a telegram telling me to report to Odyssey works for the 'Gyro' course. on Monday 15th July 1968. And to report to a Mr Eric Stevenson, in this Birkenhead facility. The course was to last a week, and it was designed to teach you how to maintain repair and operate 'Sperry' gyro's. This was a comfortable week, of easy days and early nights, just like going back to school. There were only three of us on the course and by the time we had finished the week we all felt confident with the Gyro.

There were three company ships in port,MV Cyclops, MV Stentor, and the MV Menelaus.All these ships were visited and the gyro rooms, checked out, in a real live scenario.

The following week, Monday 22nd July 1968, I reported to the Radar school at Gladstone dock, Liverpool at 0900hrs, the lecturer was Mr Waterhouse. Here we learned the in's and out's of Radar. First we learnt the principles and then the theory and hands on practical.

Practice was done on stripping down the radar scanner and attached gear boxes, this was a common problem, at sea, as I would well experience, more than once.

Then the electronics, on the bridge. We were then taken on board to witness first hand problems, that were encountered during voyages. We were furnished with much information, data and lists of parts necessary for spares on a typical voyage. Overseas suppliers and agents addresses and contacts for assistance, if necessary. No avenue was left unturned.

During the second week at the radar school at Gladstone Dock, our lecturer was Gordon Kidman. He introduced us to all the different manufacturers and types of radar used on the Alfred Holts ships, both old and new. An overview of other bridge electronics such as Auto pilot and echo sounders was also covered.

What was missing was computerisation, but then it was only 1968, but we did encounter data loggers and on the new super P's the computer controlled engine rooms. These we had to fly by the seat of our pants...

Company ships in port during those two weeks were Elpenor, Patrocolas, Aeneus Dolius and the brand new MV Peisander.

This latter ship was the subject of an extended official training visit to her spanking new engine room. Albeit very little information was available for us to learn about. Perhaps they thought it would never go wrong????

The MV Prometheus as new ready for its maiden voyage, in 1967.
Built by Vickers Ltd of Newcastle on Tyne, she ran to the Far East.
In 1974 she, along with her seven other sisters moved to 'The Barbers
Blue Sea Lines', a merger of Ocean's Blue Sea Lines and The Barber Lines,
a Wilhelmsen subsidiary in Oslo. In 1979 she was sold to CY Tung and
renamed Oriental Merchant and was converted to a cellular container ship.
She was broken up in 1986 in Kaohsiung

A diesel motor generator set is connected to the main bus-bars in the emergency generator room and connected through to the main switchboard. It provides enough power to run the ships basic requirements, lighting, heating and the galley. The installation is usually done by the shore side workers and the ships electrician switches it through when it is required.*

After completion of the radar course at Gladstone dock I went to the office in India buildings to collect my expenses and was told to report to the MV Maron that night. On arrival at the Maron, without any work gear, I wouldn't be much use, and in any case the 2nd Electrician wasn't going home till the following day, so I went home for the evening and returned 0700hrs next day, with gear, and nobody was any the wiser. Such were the intricacies of the days of life in the 'Blu Flu'... Ships in Gladstone that day were Maron, Astyanax, Pyyrhus, and the Helenus.

By Friday 9th August 1968, I had been working on the MV Maron all week and she was almost ready to start her coastal voyage to Glasgow to load cargo.

As I had the Saturday off, but had to be on duty on the Sunday, I arranged for Helen to accompany me, to Liverpool and stay on board for lunch, and dinner.

She then drove my car back home and looked after it for me.

Ships in port that week were: Atreaus, Machaon, Hector, Astyanax, and the Apapa.

Tuesday 13th August 1968 the MV Maron sailed for Glasgow, it was straight forward and we arrived at Glasgow KGV on Wednesday the 14th August at 1030hrs.

By now the routines became automatic, and I quickly learnt to get to know my fellow officers and mates on board. As crews changed regularly, time was of the essence. Recording who was who, also became automatic, as one couldn't remember all the names of the people that one met. Some guys you became buddies with and others professional friends. And sometimes it was simply 'hail fellow well met'.

The crew of the Maron were a friendly bunch.

Chief Engineer was 'Happy Knight', 2nd Engineer was Joe Barclay, Chief Electrician Andy Allen, Third Engineer Stewart Clark, 4th Engineer was Dick Martin, 5th Engineer Mike Cox.

We also had on board 8 Midshipman known as 'Middys'. 3 of them were Singaporean, with 1 Indian and 4 Europeans.

The ship was moved to Elderslie Dry Dock on the Friday 16th August 1968, so that meant more shore time as no cargo was worked in dry dock.

The MV Maron (See P005 for its history) has much attention to its hull, propeller and steering gear*

* It was always interesting to clamber into the dry dock and observe the work being done on the hull and the stern. the hull would be scraped and primed and painted, with special paint, the depth numbers would be painted back on the bows,the plimsoll lines painted amidships, the anchor chains would sometimes be completely removed with the two anchors and treated and painted.

The rudder would be inspected, its bearing surfaces checked, the stern gland would be checked, repacked as necessary, and the propeller blades would be cleaned and buffed up.

The bilge keel would be inspected, and only when all this work was complete would the ship be signed off as 'sea worthy'.

Not only did she look smart, but she would be more efficient sailing through the water.*

As a number of us had the Saturday off, it was decided to go watch Celtic play Partick thistle at Parkhead. The result I suppose was a foregone conclusion, but we enjoyed the ambience and it was an experience to see the old bars and the rivalry that the Scots are known for.

After some 'Chow' down Argyle street and of course some 'bevies' we saw this nice looking new pub just off the main street called 'The Square Peg'. Here we met up with some nice young ladies, who went by the names of Sally and Carol. And a very pleasant social evening was spent by all.

Monday morning saw the ship moved back to KG5, and preparations proceeded for an early evening departure on Tuesday for the run back to Birkenhead for cargo loading.

I duly signed off the Maron when the deep sea Electrician Frank Paterson turned up.

Ships in Vittoria dock on our arrival were Antilochus, Ajax and the Phyyrius.

On the Friday night, the 23rd August 1968 having had the evening off, plans were made with my shipboard friends Mike Cox and our girlfriends to go to watch Liverpool football club play Sunderland at Anfield stadium, on the Saturday afternoon. It was a great match.

In the evening we all had a meal in Liverpool. It had been arranged for the girls to stay in a hotel in Liverpool the 'Lord Nelson' near Lime street station. The next day Sunday I had arranged for Helen to stay on board for lunch. Mike Cox was leaving the ship, to coast the MV Machaon, and his girlfriend was going home. Also Andy Allen was leaving the ship.

Such were the movements of ships personnel. So Sunday was a very quiet day on board.

Friday the 30th August 1968 the MV Maron was scheduled to sail deep sea, so that left me 'spare'. so 'I stood by' the Myrmidon for the day. As she was about to sail also, I was told to take my accrued leave. This I did until a telegram was received. Report to Liverpool office, leave expired, Monday 23rd September 1968. On reporting to office, with gear, told to again 'stand by' MV Calchas in Kings dock Liverpool for two weeks.

On Thursday 3rd October 1968, I stood on the quayside and watched the MV Calchas sail, so I thought I may as well go home for an extended weekend, and report to the office Monday morning, which is what I did only to be told that Jimmy Quinn was on leave and to come back the following Monday, which is what I also did. Such was the nature of the job.

On reporting to Jimmy Quinn on Monday 14th October 1968, I was told to report on board the Sarpeden (ex Denbyshire) and standby until further notice.

Well this notice came by Friday 18th October 1968, from Jimmy Quinn.

Gather together your 'Deep sea gear' and join the SS Jason Gladstone dock Liverpool, due to sail noon Friday 25th October 1968, bound for Australia...

Wow, Ausy at last, couldn't be more pleased, both to get a real posting, and to get away from coasting and stand by's, for a while...

5

Australia Bound

Thursday 24th October 1968, I signed articles for the voyage to Australia, and with my 'deep sea gear' I boarded the SS Jason at Gladstone dock Liverpool.

The SS Jason, was built in 1950 by Swan, Hunter and Wigham Richardson Ltd, of Wallsend-on-Tyne, she was registered as 10,160gt's.and was an oil burning steam turbine with a service speed of 18knots, with a single propeller, delivering 15,000 SHP...

She originally was designed to carry passengers and fridge cargo, but was 'de-passengerised' in the mid 1960's. This allowed much improved accommodation for the ships officers and crew...

The SS Jason seen here passing Table Mountain, Capetown South Africa. This is a photograph of a commissioned painting by Les Cowle. I was on board at the time. 7th February 1969

Within a couple of days I made it my business to know the names of the officers with whom I would be spending the next four months, whether or not friendships grew would be another story.

Captain; JG Pettigrew, Mate; Lou Watson, 2nd mate; Howard Simpson, 3rd mate; Ron Sinclair. Chief engineer; Percy Love, 2nd engineer; John Rennie, Senior Electrician; Harry Williamson, and the Fridge man was Fred.

Ships in Gladstone Dock prior to our sailing; Priam, Sarpedon,Memnon, and Persius.

No	Name	Rank/Rating	Boat No.	Boat Duty	Emergency Party
	J.Pettigrew	Master	1	-	Bridge
	H.W.Watson	1st.Mate	2	-	A
	H.W.Simonds	2nd.Mate	3		B
	W.R.Sinclair	3rd.Mate	4	-	B
	R.Ellison	Carpenter	1	8	C
	J.Morris	Bosun	3	8	A
	W.R.Griffith	Bos' Mate	8	8	B
D1	A.McFadden	L.Seaman	1	1	B (Radio)
D2	J.Galbraith	L.Seaman	2	-	A
D3	D.Balmforth	L.Seaman	3	4 & 5	C (Lifejackets)
D7	H.D.Parry	E.D.H.	3	6 & 7	A
D8	R.P.Langford	E.D.H.	4	6 & 7	B (Lifejackets)
D4	M.C.Quinn	E.D.H.	1	4 & 5	C
D6	T.G.Trevor	E.D.H.	2	8	A
D5	M.A.Macnab	A.B.	1	4 & 5	A
D12	A.R.Mountford	J.O.S.	4	1	B
D9	J.C.Gartland	Deck Boy	1	6 & 7	A
D10	M.J.Murphy	Deck Boy	2	1	C
D13	B.Ford	Deck Boy	1	1	C
D14	A.J.Grieves	Deck Boy	3	1	R.R.
	B.R.Epps	R.O.	1	Radio	R.R.
	A.Wilcock	S.N./Purser	4	L.B.	Dispensary
	W.P.Love	Ch.Engineer	4	-	E.R.
	J.L.Rennie	2nd. "	1	8	E.R.
	F.J.Orchin	x2nd. "	2	-	E.R.
	J.McFarlane	3rd. "	2	6 & 7	E.R.
	H.B.Warren	4th. "	3	8	E.R.
	B.Cross	5th. "	4	6 & 7	E.R.
	J.Coutts	6th. "	1	6 & 7	E.R.
	H.Williamson	Sr.Electrician	4	-	E.R.
	F.Braithwaite	Jr.Electrician	1	4 & 5	E.R.
	D.Logie	Catering Offr.	4	L.B.	
	L.Woolley	2nd.Steward	1	2	
C3	J.W.Campbell	Asst.Steward	8	4 & 5	A (Lifejackets)
C4	K.Berry	Asst.Steward	3	6 & 7	A
C5	R.G.Mills	Asst.Steward	4	2	A
C2	J.A.Cox	Asst.Steward	1	3	A
C7	P.Hitching	Stews. Boy	2	6 & 7	A (Stretcher)
C6	R.W.Parker	" "	1	3	A (Stretcher)
C9	P.C.Vogel	" "	4	6 & 7	A
	D.Davis	Chief Cook	3		
	J.P.Johnson	2nd.Cook/Baker	4	4 & 5	A
C8	G.D.Lamb	Galley Boy	3	3	A
	P.A.Edmunds	Cadet Engr.	2	3	E.R.
	G.Heyes	Cadet Engr.	3	8	E.R.
	J.S.Jalland	Supernumary	4		
	H.A.Jalland	Supernumary	4		
	J.S.Rennie	Supernumary	1		
	T.R.Petticrew	Supernumary	1		
	F.D.Duffin	Cadet O'fr.	1		B
	M.F.Mallin	" "	3		Bridge
	K.A.Browne	" "	2	6 & 7	A

The official Ships register. SS Jason Voyage 48

Friday 25th October 1968, The SS Jason, fully loaded to the 'Plimsoll' line sailed down the Mersey, and passed the Bar light ship at 1330hrs, first stop Las Palmas Canary Isles, for bunkers.

The weather had been pretty foul, until arrival in The Canary Isles, on Tuesday 29th October, with rough seas and thunderstorms, and heavy rain.

Once more I was not destined to have any shore time in Las Palmas, as there were three breakdowns to be fixed. Once again the radar needed fixing as did the clear screen motor, and the 'Walkers' log. Not difficult jobs but easier done in port.

Arrival in Las Palmas was 1430hrs, for full bunkers and water and of course the mail. All the problems were sorted by our departure time of 0200hrs, 29th October.

The Glenogle was also in port taking full bunkers. The temperature was a close and cloudy 24C...

Thursday 31st October I put on a film show, for the officers and crew in the dining saloon. It was a James bond film 'You only live twice' 007 films were always popular, and we had a good turn out and all enjoyed it with a few beers also.* The electrician always put the film shows on, on board*.

Weather was good and we were into 'whites' today. Due to cross the equator today at1400hrs, Sunday 3rd November 1968. We passed the Glengarry, homeward bound, with the customary sounding of the hooters and well wishes on the RT.With a warning of bad weather around the Cape.

By Friday 8th November the weather had turned foul again, we were back in blues, and a force 8 gale had whipped up.We passed the Peisander and the Clytonius, homeward bound, with warnings from both of them of bad weather around the Cape.

It was in fact a head on force 8/9 and we had to heave too and secure stays and guy ropes forward. We reduced revs, to avoid over revving the engine, as the weather was getting worse. 30 foot waves over the bows, so life lines were issued and great care had to be taken.

The outer reaches of Capetown were entered Sunday 10th November 1968 and we were alongside in berth 'B', next to the 'Edinburgh Castle' by 0800hrs. I went ashore for a quick look around, but couldn't go far, as there was work to be done before we sailed again the following morning by 0630hrs…

We left Capetown, 0630hrs, Monday 11th November 1968, for Melbourne.

No sooner had we left the confines of the harbour, when the foul weather hit us, head on force 9.Water everywhere, causing 'earths' on my switchboard faster than I could clear them.

Again we hove too to check all watertight doors and guy lines and winch cables.

The ship was losing bits off her, being washed overboard, on waking up the following morning, in the cold light of day the damage sustained was evident.

The port side of the bridge was ripped to shreds, together with the port navigation lights and

over side lights and boat lights.The promenade deck hand rails, and front storm windows were all bent and stove in, and the lounge windows smashed. this caused the lounge to be flooded, together with the alleyways, and the port stairways were washed away.

The gale has been blowing all day and it takes one all ones strength and energy to do any normal chores let alone do any work.

By Sunday morning 17th November 1968, the wind seemed to be stronger and at 1530hrs a massive wave hit us on the port side, whilst we were in a trough of rollers, and smashed all the port side bulkhead doors, flooding the alleyways and cabins.

We had to 'hove too' again and make temporary repairs.

Whilst these repairs were in hand I received a message from the Captain. 'Eh Braithwaite, could you possibly rig up a temporary Port side navigation light??' 'Aye sir' I replied.

I went up to the bridge to speak to the Captain and said, 'And where would you like me to put it sir??' Bearing in mind that the Port side bridge wing was now just matchsticks. 'Just do what you can Braithwaite, do what you can'. 'Aye Aye sir' I said.

And with that I strapped on my life line and went in search of the 'Chippy'. On finding him I explained that I wanted some sort of beam to be lashed roughly where the bridge wing would be and on the end of it I would affix a temporary Navigation light. this was done and between us the Navigation light was fixed in place, albeit very roughly, but sturdily, and a cable was linked into the wheelhouse and secured and connected to the broken supply. Job done.

By the Monday 19th November 1968, the seas had calmed down somewhat but it was still cold and windy and we seemed to be rolling more than usual. We also seemed to have a bit of a list, which we compensated for by pumping deep tanks from starboard to Port. Better but not correct. It was later found that the cargo had shifted. When we opened up the hatches in Melbourne we found a lot of twisted metal that was once many hundreds of 'Land Rovers'.

All across the Australian 'bight', as we rolled a heavy grinding noise was evident, and it was later discovered that our bilge keel had been damaged and was loose.

All these problems, took its toll on the ship, and we were losing time on our schedule, and as one knows, time is money.

But even worse for the company was the damaged cargo and the further loss of time, as it would be evident that a dry docking would have to be done somewhere in Australia before our homeward journey.

Arrival in Melbourne was on 27th November 1968 at 1800hrs, almost two days later than scheduled, it was warm and very dry and windy. We were however, glad to be out of the Australian Bight and tied up in port again, we were at the South quay, berth 32. And cargo handling and discharge began in earnest.

Arrangements were also being made for a dry docking in Darling harbour, Sydney, on our arrival.The ship would need some considerable repair to make her ship-shape again...

Meanwhile, Ron Sinclair, Frank Duffin, and a number of us went ashore for a few beers at the London Hotel, followed by a meal in an Italian restaurant and a few more beers, it was so good to set foot on 'terra firma' again.

Melbourne was a modern city not unlike New York, but dead as a do-do. They have large skyscrapers and apartment blocks and stores and flashing signs and lights. but getting there needed a taxi, it was some considerable distance from berth 32, but well worth the visit.

Everything was very expensive by our standards, but the old trams and the railway station were very interesting places, by the look of it. But that would be for another day. It was back to the ship and back to work sorting out some of the damaged gear as best we could...

As we were expected to be in Melbourne for at least a week, it wasn't all work, and on the Saturday 7th December, a party was organised for us by the local nurses.

So, Ron Sinclair, Frank Duffin, myself and most of the cadets and midis went ashore to this party. We had a great time, it was a pyjama party, with great company, fun and food and drink. Met a lovely girl called Jennie, immediately took a shine to her, and made sure that I could see her again. As a foursome we spent the Sunday afternoon in the Botanical gardens in Melbourne, followed by a run by car down the coast to Geelong, a pretty seaside village.

The Melbourne Trams, in Late 1968. Both these photos are of the 'W' class Melbourne tram first introduced in 1923, which were to become an Icon of the MMTB. These trams ran well into the 1970's when the 'Z' class was introduced

Monday 9th December 1968

We left Melbourne for the last time this voyage, at 1830hrs Ausy time. Due Sydney 0500hrs 11th December.

Wednesday 11th December 1968

We arrived at Sydney at 0730hrs.

What a magnificent city, we anchored out and had a superb view of the harbour. It's so much like Hong Kong, with its new huge buildings, its magnificent "Coat Hanger Bridge" and strange looking theatre, which looked like three upturned ships on end. The weather was glorious, 25C and sun shining. The houses and apartments on the North or 'well-to-do side' of Sydney look select and delightful, many of them coming down to the water's edge. There are all sorts of craft roaming around the harbour, ferries galore, together with ships and a hydrofoil to Manly beach. It looks a place of character and interest.

During a great night ashore, Saturday 14th December, I met a girl called Ann, she was a student from Sydney University. We seemed to get on well, so I arranged to see her the next afternoon, she showed me Manly beach where we went swimming, surfing and 'bronzying'. She seemed to know a lot of the guys on the beach, and soon we were playing beach volleyball, and having a great time. However we had to return to the ship as some of us had watches and work to be done. However I arranged to see her again on the Monday afternoon. the 16th, this I had to alter, as work intervened.

Tuesday 17th December 1968

I had the afternoon off, so I took a walk uptown, through the Botanic gardens, Hyde Park, down Elizabeth street, to railway square. I saw the old Government house, it looked like an old English castle, with battlements. It flew the British Union Jack, and had lodges at the main and side gates.

The P&O passenger liner the SS Orcades, seen here at the passenger liner terminal at Darling Harbour, Sydney, she was built in 1947 by Vickers Armstrongs. in Barrow-in -Furness, and was designed as a Royal mail passenger Liner for the UK- Australia- New Zealand route, and was used for first class and tourist class passengers as well as immigrants. She was taken out of service in 1972 and sent to the breakers yards in Kaohsiung in 1973

The old Government house in Sydney. This house is a Vice Regal residence of the Governor of New South Wales Australia, located alongside The Botanical Gardens. It is a listed building built in 1847 in the Gothic Revival style

The flower gardens were beautiful, full of big red irises. In the Botanic gardens the different trees were fascinating, the Ausy eucalyptus, the palms and desert cactus and there was a bottle tree from New Zealand, so called because it looked like a bottle, with leaves sprouting out of the top.

This view of the Sydney Harbour Bridge and newly built Opera House is from the Botanical Gardens

The ponds were full of yellow and red lilies and teeming with fish. From here I walked past Woollamalloo, to Hyde Park crossing the modern approaches to the 'coat hanger bridge'. On the left was the Art Gallery and museum, a grand old buildings like the Library in Lime street Liverpool, with huge pillars and columns and sandstone carvings and tapestries. I walked past the fountain in Hyde Park, where tomorrow's Sydney's marathon cars will rally for there so called 'lap of honour'. Unfortunately we will miss that as we are due to sail at midnight tonight, for Port Kembla.

The Sydney City Cathedral, also of the Gothic Revival Style, designed by William Wardell in 1821, is the Cathedral church of the Roman Catholic Archdiocese and the seat of the current Archbishop of Sydney, Anthony Fisher OP

From here I looked at the cathedral and the war memorial and on past the city bowling club, where they were all dressed in their white trousers and boaters and all took the game very seriously.

I turned right and then left again down Elizabeth street to the goods, parcel and carriage cleaning plants of the central station in Railway Square. Here I saw many wonderful steam engines, 4-6-4tanks, 4-4-0's (3305). I talked to a railway guy, who told me that the buildings were over a hundred years old, 1865. I then walked up to the station and was delighted to see two Australian Railway pacific class 4-6-2 semi streamlined locos, No's 3810 and 3811, along with 6 shunting locos as well as modern diesel and electric locos. I spent a couple of hours just watching them and taking in the ambience before making my way back to the ship, via George street, past Wynyard station and Circular Quay.

An old steam engine still in use in the parcels bay in Sydney station in 1968. She was a 2-6-4 tank loco built by Beyer Peacock and Co between 1903 and 1917. There were 145 originally built and 5 now survive in various states of preservation. The engine seen here survived until 1973

After a shower and supper, I rang Ann to see how her first day at work had been. It was good to speak to her again although I had to tell her that we were sailing at midnight and that I would contact her again on our return run.

I then decided to get my head down for a few hours as stand-by was at midnight.

We sailed at midnight with my mate and myself perched precariously on top of the radar scanner repairing the gears again, this gave us a great view of the underside of the Sydney harbour bridge, we were close enough to count every rivet, as we sailed beneath it, and by the time we reached the heads we had the radar fixed and running sweetly again.

In about three hours we were due in Port Kembla, South of Sydney, so it was decided that it would be hardly worth getting cleaned up and going to bed.

0220hrs 18th December 29.98 inches, barometer steady, 69degrees F, humidity 81 percent, expected noon high 82F. Radio 2UV Sydney.

So with a coffee and a 'cig' we awaited the early morning standby, and took in the views and approaches of Port Kembla.

18th December 1968 Wednesday Radio Woollangong.

Arrived at Port Kembla at anchor 0445hrs. Scheduled to go alongside this afternoon.

Due to leave Friday 20th, but it maybe later as one derrick had to be sent ashore for repair due to a snapped stay wire. And that was not the only subject that had to go ashore.

It just so happened that when that stay wire snapped and the derrick came crashing down, my colleague and fellow officer Harry Williamson and I were working on deck, and Harry was directly in the line of that falling derrick, so I, instinctively, did a flying rugby tackle on Harry, pushing him out of the line of the falling derrick. This possibly saved him from being killed, or seriously injured, but in doing so we both landed on the side on the hatch combing and the fall broke Harry's arm. So a trip to hospital in Port Kembla was necessary for Harry. This would also restrict him from his work for the rest of the trip, and meant more work for me also. But at least he was still alive and the arm would mend.

We Sailed from Port Kembla, 21st December 1968 Saturday, 0730hrs, due Newcastle, at reduced revs, at approx 1600hrs.

Arrived at 1600hrs, Newcastle, what a super little place, great beaches and town and weather.

This steam crane tank engine was a rare find, usually to be found in stores or works environments, and was most certainly built circa 1900. No 1067 was built in 1923 by Hawthorne Lesley as works no L041 and is still in existence at The Dorrigo Steam Railway and Museum in New South Wales Australia. Technically these crane engines were 'Luffing Crane Tank Locomotives' with a maximum lift of 7 tons'

Monday 23rd December 1968

Due to sail 0220hrs for Sydney, due to arrive 0430hrs, at reduced revs, 14 knots, to pick up the pilot.

We arrived at Sydney on Christmas Eve, Tuesday 24th December 1968 at 0430hrs. We picked up the pilot, and proceeded straight into dry dock in Darling harbour.

The ship spent the next 10days in dry dock, having structural repairs, to the hull, keel and superstructure after our bad sea voyage across the Indian and Australian bight.

This enabled me to spend Christmas day ashore but I was on duty for New Years day.

On Christmas eve arrangements were made to meet Ann and a crowd of us, including Ron Sinclair and Frank Duffin, went to a night club called the 'Whisky Agogo', and after a few beers and some super seafood, plenty of dancing and fun, a great time was had by all.

I was very fortunate to be invited to Ann's family home Christmas Day., and over the Christmas period, where I met her family, brother's John 17, Robert 16, and sister Wendy 13. Also her mum and dad and grandparents.I stayed until 0200hrs on the 27th December, before having to return to the ship, a memorable Christmas.Their hospitality was second to none, and what's more I enjoyed their company.

However, it was my duty on over the New year. We let the New Year in, in style on board, with superb food and plenty of beer and fun and a good old sing song.

The following day, New Years day, I was invited again to spend it with the Harrison family,

We drove up to the Blue mountains, where we saw the results of the summer bush fires, near Katoomba, and the majestic Three Sisters, very hot and dry but a spectacular mountain range.

We all said our farewells on the Sunday afternoon/evening not just to Sydney, but to all the lovely people that we had met, and sailed for Brisbane at midnight.

It was now the Saturday, 11th January 1969, the temperature was 98F, with 82% humidity and it was sunny and bright, as we docked in Brisbane.

Ron Sinclair, Frank Duffin, myself and half a dozen others organised to go on a coach tour from Southport to Coolangatta down the Gold Coast, on the Sunday.

It was a super trip, good food, drink and company, and we saw the wonders of the Gold Coast and the Great Barrier Reef, at its Southern most point near Fraser Island.

All too brief but it gave us an insight, into its wonders.

During the week I had much work to catch up on and much standby for loading cargo.

Also much sleep to catch up on, as it was very hot and humid.

We left Brisbane at 2200hrs Saturday 12th January 1969 and were full away by 0330hrs. It was good to get to sea again with some fresh air, and especially as it was now homeward bound.

We tested the steering gear, and dropped the lifeboats for emergency boat drill.

As usual I was elected to go aboard the lifeboat. The Jason disappeared over the horizon and we did all the necessary tests, all went well and the Jason returned and we were hoisted aboard again.

We sailed around the South of Australia to Albany WA arrival was 0930hrs and we intended to work cargo for whale oil.

After waiting for 24hrs, on this day, Saturday 25th January 1969, for the wind to abate, to allow the pipeline to be floated out to us, it took only some 10hrs to load the precious cargo, and we immediately sailed for Capetown, South Africa, expected 12 days hence weather permitting.

During the crossing of the Southern Indian ocean I spent many 8 to 12 evening watches on the bridge with Ron Sinclair, the 3rd mate, we would discuss the good times and the girls we had met in Australia and generally put the world to rights.

I also learnt all I know about navigation and good seamanship from Ron at the same time.

Saturday 1st February 1969

The crossing otherwise was pretty uneventful, weather was good, 85degF and sunny each day.

The sunset tonight was particularly beautiful, as the sun dipped below the horizon, a splash of red covered everything, and it was raining well to our stern, and the rainbow was stunning and complete.

Land was sighted today, Wednesday 5th February 1969

Great. South Africa.East London. We then travelled South to Capetown.

SS Jason seen here docked in Capetown South Africa 7th February 1969

By Friday 7th February 1969,

we Arrived at Capetown, at 0530hrs

When we docked the MV Rotterdam was next to us.

Went ashore with the camera, took many photos in the city and the Railway Station and the dock areas. I saw many steam engine types and recorded them for posterity.

We sailed from Capetown, 1730hrs for Flushing Holland, due 24th.

Wednesday 12th February 1969

For days now there has been no winds and the currents have been with us, we are making good way, but my, is it hot and humid, cabin is too hot to sleep in 95degF so am sleeping outside on the deck.The doldrums. smooth as a mill pond. passed many fishing vessels, near the Gulf of guinea, also MV Maron, MV Astyanax and MV Glen Finlass all outward bound.

Will be glad to get home now.

Sunday 16th February 1969

Today is much cooler, and then at 0500hrs, suddenly thick fog. standby was rung, we were just off Freetown, North West Africa. All clear and full away by 0900hrs.

Tuesday 18th February 1969

2000hrs, just off Mauritania, 'sparks' received a real SOS from just North of the Bay of Biscay. We are too far off to help, other vessels are in attendance.

The weather here just off Las Palmas, is worsening to fairly rough, windy but still warm.

Saturday 22nd February 1969

Now halfway across the Bay of Biscay, weather cool but good.

Sunday 23rd February 1969

This morning we rounded the channel, past Guernsey, We are well and truly in the English Channel now, ships all around us, BBC programs on VHF bands available, much catching up of the local news. ETA Flushing 0200hrs, revs down to 78 still doing 14 knots, weather cool, 45 to 50F, Visibility good.

Monday 24th February 1969

Temperature dropped quite suddenly in the channel during the night, and the seas changed from blue to grey, and on arrival at Flushing it was a mere 36F. Standby for Flushing was 0200hrs. FWE (Finished with engines) was 0630hrs.

We hope to be away from Flushing by 2000hrs.

Standby was, if fact 2000hrs, 24th, but fog persisted all the way up the English channel, but we arrived outside the North Canada dock wall, Liverpool, at 1130hrs today. Wednesday 26th February 1969.

We were due to go alongside the Polythemus at 1800hrs, maybe able to get away early the following morning.

I said my goodbyes to Ron and Frank and the guys and wished them a good leave.Some were staying on and coasting, others were joining other ships, and some like me were due some leave.

Thursday 28th February 1969

Helen was on the dockside by 1100hrs ready to collect me and take me home.

Voyage 48 was complete. I had experienced life in Australia, made many friends and met many lovely people and made a life time friend in Ron Sinclair, he was, and always will be my 2nd brother., But alas, he has, at the time of writing this missive, 'crossed the bar', RIP shipmate.

And now for a spot of leave, some six weeks were due.

6

A Period of Changes and Promotion

After some 6 weeks leave, I received a telegram to report to the office in Liverpool, on Monday 14th April 1969, at 1000hrs.

After a hint that I was about to get promotion, to Senior Electrician soon, I was officially told that day that my promotion had come through.

So one of many changes to my life had happened, necessitating a visit to 'Holts Mutual' for the upgrade to my uniform. Another stripe.And of course more money.

Another even bigger change to my life occurred during my leave when Helen and I decided to get engaged to be married, although no date had been set for that event, as we would, as you did, in those days, save your money and collect things for the 'bottom draw'.

This change in one's lifestyle necessitated much thought as to if, and how much longer, I would remain in the Merchant Navy as a sea going engineer, as to put it bluntly, why get married if you were not together. So I decided that by the end of the year, December 1969, or thereabouts, I would need to be looking at a shore based job, sufficient to support us, as a married couple.

Anyway I digress.

After I had organised the upgrade to my uniform, I was to report to the MS Daru in Brunswick dock, Liverpool, to assist Bill Driver for a couple of days.

The MS Daru was quite a nice ship, well looked after and tidy.and Bill and myself got on well, both of us knew what we were doing, and got the jobs done quickly. But by Thursday 17th April, I was to report to the office again for further instructions.

I was needed in London, and could I 'nip' down there and relieve a Mr Jones on the Onitsha when it docked...

To that end I collected my gear, my travel warrants and called for Helen at work and then drove to Manchester Piccadilly station. After a coffee, I said my goodbyes and caught the10-27hrs train to London. I hailed a taxi at Euston to take me to Tilbury and arrived at the MV Eboe at about 1600hrs. This was to be my overnight accommodation until the next day when the Onitsha was due to dock.

The MV Onitsha, Tilbury Docks London, 19th April 1969. Built in 1952, at Harland and Wolf, Belfast for Elder Dempster Lines and taken over by Ocean Fleets in 1965 was sold on to a Cyprus shipping Co, in 1972

The Onitsha arrived at berth 10/11 of Tilbury docks at 1400hrs, on Saturday 19th April1969, and shortly afterwards Mr Jones left after a short handover, and I looked over the ship. A well looked-after ship, but with much work to be done.

Time was spent on the Sunday fixing two winches, in readiness for cargo working on the Monday morning. One repair entailed the relining of the winch brake.

Other ED ships in dock that day were the Patani, Ebani and of course the Eboe on which I had stayed the night before.

The Beautiful Ellerman Line Ship 'City of Auckland' in Tilbury Docks 27th April 1969. Built by Vickers Armstrong Barrow-in-Furness in 1956 as a refrigerated cargo ship, sold on to Gulf Shipping Lines Ltd in 1978, and broken up in Bombay in 1983

Today Sunday 27th April was spent on a site-seeing trip into London, from St Katharines Wharf and Tower Bridge to Westminster Cathedral. Also saw the Maritime Museum, unfortunately it was closed, Greenwich, The War Museum and The Cutty Sark. An Interesting monument in London was the Merchant Navy and Fishing Fleets Monument., which can be found on Tower Hill ...

The Merchant Navy and Fishing Fleets Monument in Tower Hill London. The memorial was designed by Sir Edward Lutyens and unveiled on the 12 December 1928 by Queen Mary, to commemorate the lives of the Merchant Seaman who have no graves but the sea

Returning to the ship for dinner and a pleasant evening playing cards and having a few beers, with the 4th Engineer, Chris Page...

As the MV Onitsha was due to sail from Tilbury Wednesday 14th May and Mr Jones was back on board, my orders were to return to Birkenhead and stand by the MV Nelius for the day and then take a week's leave...Dave Varley was the senior electrician on board, and assistance was given to him for the day.

During my weeks leave, I decided the time was approaching for a change of occupation, not just for personal reasons, but to keep up with the ever-changing modern thinking of the day.

Although Blue Funnel was a great company, they were old fashioned, which I liked, but in practice, their time was numbered. Their attempts to move with the times were not fast enough for me and I decided that I must resign before the end of the year, 1969.

I knew that I would be held to a three months notice period, so planning when to resign was important, as in all probability I would or could be sent on a three or four month deep sea voyage.

To that end, on my next visit to the office, I explained this and my reasoning to my Superintendent Jimmy Quinn. Now I always found and had the greatest respect for him, as he would always hear you out and logically reason with you and advise you, not just as an employer, but in a fatherly way. But he would never 'beat about the bush', and what he said usually made good sense.

He said that he understood and concurred with my reasoning, but would hold my resignation until I had completed at least one deep sea voyage as senior electrician, as this he said would prove my credibility as an engineer, and give me that bit more experience, that would give me a more comprehensive CV, for future employment.

He also confided in me saying that he tended to agree with me on the future of Blue Funnel, and that he felt that his days were numbered, and that he was coming up for retirement.

As a man of his word, I knew that he would do as he said, as I trusted him implicitly. My next orders were to report to the MV Ajax in London, Surrey commercial docks, Finland yard, and to relieve the incoming Senior Electrician Bill Craig. I arrived on board at 1500hrs, on Wednesday 28th May 1969, the ship was handed over to me and Bill Craig was on his way home, on leave.

The ship's accommodation was very spacious and well appointed, all planned maintenance was up to date and she was 'ship shape and Bristol fashion'.

The Ajax was semi automated and had a notorious gas turbine emergency generator.

Sailing was to be at 0130hrs, 3rd June 1969, for dry docking in Avonmouth with onward cargo loading at Swansea.

Departure from Avonmouth was 2000hrs 13th June 1969, arriving at Swansea and anchoring out to await the tide.

During our stay in Swansea I walked up the valleys, to see how the Welsh boys lived, visited a church, and went to the 'Castle Cinema' in town during the evening, to see a film. The town was all very quiet.

Departure from Swansea, was 1700hrs 18th June on a beautiful sunny evening, steaming past the Mumbles and on to Liverpool.

By Sunday 28th June the Ajax had transferred to Birkenhead, and was working cargo flat out

and I was on 24hrs cargo watch. There were no major problems, and by Monday morning the deep sea senior electrician, Bill Craig was back, that released me and I reported to the office the next morning, Tuesday 1st July 1969.

Today was the investiture of Prince Charles at Caernarvon Castle, as the Prince of Wales.

Although I had some time to watch the ceremony, I was preparing for the trip to London on Friday the 4th July, when I would be joining the MV Aeneas to do a 'Home Trade' coasting.

The 1030hrs train from Manchester Piccadilly took me to London Euston, then a taxi to Surrey Commercial Canada Docks and I was on board by1500hrs, reporting to the then Senior Electrician, Hugh Stewart, who after the customary handover, was away home on leave. I spent the rest of the day finding my way around the ship and meeting the few officers and crew that were still there.

During the next week the MV Aeneas was unloaded and we were ready to sail to Avonmouth by 11th July, for further unloading.

We were away from London by 2200hrs, and down the Thames estuary and FSA by 0730hrs the next morning, arriving at anchor by Avonmouth by 1000hrs and alongside by 1900hrs on Sunday 13th July 1969.

It was a beautiful summers evening and the docks were quiet, it was quite eerie. There was not a lot of work done that week as the dockers were on a 'work to rule'.

This was the beginning of the end for the British Merchant Navy...

The country was brought to the verge of a national strike by Arthur Scargill, and caused innumerable repercussions, through-

The MV Ajax in Avonmouth Dry Dock in June 1969. She was the last 'A' boat to be built for A/H by Vickers Armstrong Ltd of Newcastle upon Tyne in 1958, and was renamed Deucalion in 1972. In 1973 she was sold to the Nan Yang Shipping Co, and was again renamed Kailok, and was broken up in Kaohsiung in 1982

The MV Aeneas in Tilbury Docks, London in 1969. The MX Aeneas was built at the Caledon shipbuilders and Co Ltd of Dundee in 1947 and gave a full service under the big blue funnel until it was sent to the breakers yards in Kaohsiung in 1972

out British industry, and this included the dock workers etc. Hence Blue Funnel tried to get as many of their ships away overseas, as soon as possible, as harbour dues and overheads cost money.

We departed Avonmouth Saturday 19th July and were due to 'lock-in' at Liverpool the following day at 0430hrs. The weather was misty and there was a long swell in the Irish sea, with a force 8 gale forecast, we made all haste to outrun it.

We docked in Liverpool shortly after 0500hrs on the 20th July 1969, and after working cargo for a couple of days, I signed off the MV Aeneas 24th July 1969.

On contacting the office I was told to go on a week's leave and prepare for a 'deep sea' voyage.

It was during this week's leave that yet another change to my life would be decided. And this time it was the biggest decision that was ever to be made, to date. Helen and I were to be married, before I went deep sea, as it would be the middle of the winter by the time that I returned, and my resignation would then be imminent. So the date was set for the marriage ceremony to be on the 30th July 1969.

However all was not so straight forward. My leave was due up on the 28th July. So I had to go to the office and tell Jimmy Quinn the story, and ask for some leave 'in lieu'.

He was prepared to go along with this, as the MV Anchises was not due to sail from Birkenhead until Friday the 8th August 1969, on the understanding that I sign articles from the 29th July1969 and be prepared for deep sea and be prepared to receive a telegram, at short notice to join the ship...This was agreed, between Jimmy and myself. All I had to do now was tell Helen. Wow, why did life have to be so complicated??

Well we were married, in church, on the 30th July 1969, and it all went without a hitch, and we had a honeymoon in 'The Queens Hotel' in Llandudno, albeit shorter than planned due to a certain telegram, telling me to report to the MV Anchises. I then took a deep breath.

EUROPEAN CREW LIST.

Ref.No.	Name.	Rank.	Dis.A.No.	Place of Birth.	D.O.B.
1.	Leslie Haldane POUND	Master	LO.140281	Blackpool	18-1-24
2.	John BRUNSKILL	Mate	R.579607	Blackburn	8-12-34
3.	Anthony Hardstaff MEASURES	Snr.2nd Mate	R.685483	Blackpool	19-1-41
4.	John Colmcille GILLESPIE	2nd Mate	E.3944	Bunbeg	30-3-42
5.	Bernard Eden Mansel THOMAS	3rd Mate	R.814607	Penrith	21-5-48
6.	Randal MAGOWAN	R.O.	R.708823	Stockport	22-5-40
7.	Thomas Arthur MOORE	Ch.Engr.	R.590467	Liverpool	23-7-32
8.	Paul Cyril BLANCHARD	2nd Engr.	R.807481	Grimsby	2-2-43
10.	John Arthur TAYLOR	4th Engr.	R.849834	Long Eaton	18-2-43
11.	Robert Lyn ATACK	Asst.Engr.	R.865751	Barrow in Furness	3-8-46
12.	Michael DODGSON	Asst.Engr.	R.865749	Barrow in Furness	3-7-46
13.	Thomas Leslie REEVES	Asst.Engr.	R.871578	Liverpool	29-5-48
14.	Philip Anthony BRAITHWAITE	Snr.Elect.	R.848947	Warrington	18-3-44
15.	John Thomas DOYLE	Cat.Offr.	R.533142	Liverpool	29-5-34
16.	George Henry HARLOCK	Engr.Cadet	R.871653	Limavady	14-10-50
17.	Charles Ronald ORRITT	Engr.Cadet	R.871659	Ormskirk	5-8-51
18.	WONG Kok Choi	3rd Engr.	SI.13283	Kedah	21-7-42
-	Jonathan Michael Desmond PERRY	Offr.Cadet	R.845608	Dublin	17-9-50

Total European Crew : 18

............................f...Master.

The MV Anchises in Royal docks London. Built by the Caledon shipbuilding Co Ltd of Dundee in 1947, after many years under A/H she was transferred to NSMO and renamed MV Alcinous, then to China Mutual. In 1974 she briefly went to Glen line before reverting back to China mutual. In late 1975 she was sent to the breakers yards in Kaohsiung. A table of the crew. The European crew numbered 18 and the Chinese 34

This was to be my last deep sea voyage, the MV Anchises and as a Senior Electrician.

By 1800hrs on the 6th August 1969 I was on board the ship at Birkenhead. She was fully provisioned and loaded and we sailed on schedule at 1800hrs the 8th August 1969 with FSA by 2345hrs, first stop Las Palmas Canary Isles...

As we left Liverpool I saw the Llandudno to Holyhead ferry, and it only seemed like five minutes ago that I was in Llandudno on my honeymoon, and yet here I was sailing away to the Far East, on a voyage that could last over four months.

It didn't take long before the realities that were ships life set in, with our first 'scavenge fire' on No;2 unit. It was soon dealt with and we still maintained our ETA Las Palmas of 0600hrs 13th August...The weather was glorious, warm, calm and blue, into 'Whites' today.

We collected mail and full bunkers at Las Palmas, our departure at 1730hrs heralded the entry of MV Menestheus, homeward bound.

As we passed the Dakar lighthouse, the MV Pelius passed us also homeward bound, with the customary exchange of hooters we both went our separate directions.

Tuesday 19th August 1969, the ship crossed the equator, it was decidedly cool and windy and cloudy and during the early hours of the following morning we had yet another scavenge fire, this time on No's 6 and 7 and spreading to 8, before we had it under control...

By Friday 22nd August we picked up our first albatross, which latched on to us for the remainder of the Atlantic to Capetown. what huge majestic birds they are and those beady eyes stare at you all the time...

As we arrived at anchor in Capetown, all the lights were a-twinkling round table mountain, and around the coast.For once the sea was calm and the air warm, it would have been nice to go ashore there, but alas not this time, and after the mail was collected and ours sent, we were FSA for Penang, by 2100hrs Monday 25th August 1969.

By Wednesday the 27th a gale force 8 had sprung up, and the old girl was shipping copious amounts of sea water on board, especially in the windlass room up for'ward, and she was pitching and rolling, necessitating reduced revs again.

However that didn't stop me putting on a film show that evening. It was called 'The Guns of Patasi', a good film, a Western, with lots of humour in it. It went down well...

Saturday night was 'The Point to Point', and as the weather had calmed down a bit, we had a good turn out and as bookies agent most of my clients showed a small prophet. 10% going to charity naturally.

This run from Capetown to Penang was always a long drag, it was plus/minus 33 days, and keeping ones spirits up was always a challenge, particularly if the weather and seas were rough, and to some, a journey a bit too far. When the sea was calm, we used to play cricket on the forward well deck, you can imagine how many balls went over the side, lost to the oceans, in two days we lost 48 balls, still we all had a good laugh, and it was good exercise.

Those last few days before Penang were always challenging, the heat of the approaching tropics, the lack of good sleeping weather, the deterioration in the quality of the food.

This invariably caused irritability and frayed tempers.

On Friday the 6th September, I put on another film for the crew, it was a western called 'The Plunderers', and on the Saturday, I did bar duty, to give the No1 steward a night off.It was a busy night as I think the whole ship had a skin full that night. Such was the mood of the ship...

Arrival at Penang was 1100hrs on the 10th September 1969, with the temperatures well into the 90's. we tied up alongside, the pilot departed and the ship prepared to unload its cargo.

Cargo was worked for 2 days before departure for Port Swettenham, on the Friday at 1700hrs.

I ventured ashore to stretch the legs, walking along the sea front, and through the town, It was very quiet that day and the air was still and humid.

The old Colonial style building in Penang, this was the City Hall.. It is the headquarters of the local government in Georgetown Penang Malaysia. It was built in 1902 and is part of a 'Unesco' world heritage site, overlooking the parade ground (or Padang) within the esplanade.

We sailed for Port Swettenham, at 1700 hrs on the evening of the 12th September, arriving and working cargo for 1 day before sailing for Singapore, at 1700hrs on the 13th September.

We were minus the 3rd engineer, Kok Choi Wong, when we sailed.

As he was a Singapore citizen, one can only assume he went missing for family reasons, with or without permission, unknown, but he was on the quayside on our arrival in Singapore.

Arrival in the Western roads was 0600hrs Sunday 14th September 1969. We went alongside, berth1/2, Keppel Harbour, in a tropical rainstorm, visibility only some 5 yards, quite tricky. The Rhexenor followed us alongside some two hours later.

The following day the 15th September 1969, I went ashore, primarily to do some shopping, returning for a party on board arranged by the mate, John Brunskill, with some 11 nurses from 'The British Military Hospital'.

Jack Doyle, our catering officer laid on some party food and No1steward and myself served at the bar, Sparks, Randal Magowan, provided the music.They were very pleasant girls and we all partied and danced the night away...

First light on the Tuesday morning, I was awakened to be told that my presence was required to make up a foursome on the Keppel golf course with the Captain, Chief Engineer and Jack Doyle. You don't argue with such a request, and so the golf course it was to be, I borrowed a set of clubs and oft we went. All very Colonial and British, complete with caddies and a drinks trolley. Then back to the 19 tee for drinks and lunch, all on the Captain, of course. Well one had to do these things, didn't one...

We sailed from Singapore at 1630hrs, and as we went down the Eastern roads, company ships in port were MV Aeneas, Stentor and the Centaur. What a magnificent ship the Centaur is, pure white with a blue stripe, from bow to stern, above the green boot topping, and the super 'P' funnel three quarter aft. We also sailed with two stowaways, on board.

An Englishman and a Siamese 'Fairy', both off the SS Ixion, and being returned to Bangkok. Both were locked in separate cabins for the trip. What next???

Arrival at anchorage for Bangkok was 2000hrs Friday, 19th September 1969, moving up to our berth No:1 on Saturday at 1600hrs.

*The **SS Steel Director in Bangkok in 1969, tied up alongside another ship.
She was built for the Istmian Lines, by Ingalis Shipbuilding Corporation in
Pascagoula MS in 1944 and was classified as a C3 general cargo Victory boat.*

On Sunday 21st September we had a visit from the Captain of
the ship berthed next to us...

His ship, the SS Steel Director, of the Isthmian Lines, a C3
general cargo Victory boat, was in trouble. She had 'blacked
out' as he put it, after a winch had jammed, and created a dead
short across the generators, causing them to stall, apparently.
When they ran the generators up again, they would not supply
any power. Now he did not have an electrician on board, and
the engineers had no idea what had happened and what to do
about it. Did we have an electrician on board that could come
over and help us??, as he had already lost a day's cargo working.

I said that I would have to speak to my chief, Tom Moore,
which I did, and he said, "OK, go over and check it out, take the
2nd Engineer, Paul Blanchard, but report back to me before you
do anything."

This we did. Well what a mess that ship was... No power, no
lighting or ventilation working.

After reporting back to our chief engineer, we got the go ahead to do what we could, but to take great care, as it was a potentially hazardous situation, and we were not signed on any articles for that ship and should there be any repercussions, we must not be held responsible, and an agreement was entered into, between the Captain and the Chief Engineer.

Firstly we ascertained what deck equipment was responsible for the initial problem, and isolated two winches from the switch board.

Then working in 15minute intervals, (could only breathe safely for that time down on the engine flats, as there was no lighting, ventilation or power) we ascertained the engine room layout and the position of the switchboard. There was one inboard and one outboard steam turbine powered generator. They had both been running when the incident happened and both suffered severe 'arcing' damage across the commutators.

There was also a small diesel powered generator on the engine flat, but the diesel engine was down having work done on its engine.

So the commutators would have to be fixed if possible.

All the brushes were lifted and some had to be replaced. Fortunately, they had some spares.

All the breakers on the switchboard were tripped, and isolated. One bus bar at a time was disconnected on the steam turbine powered generator, and the integrity of the stator was checked with our trusty 'mega' all ok. reconnected. They fortunately had enough steam to turn the rotor to enable me to clean up the commutator, and then undercut the segments, to ensure that there was no further shorting at the commutator. This done all the brushes were reseated on the commutator and the engine then 'run up' again, with no load.Voltage checked 120 volts ok (USA had a voltage of 110 to 120 volts), Essential breakers brought in one by one, all ok.

The same procedure was done on the other steam turbine powered generator, and we were back in business. All that remained to be done was that the winches, which had caused the original problem, would have to be fixed by their engineers before they could be used again.

Job done... and now for a 'few' beers... We reported back to our chief engineer, and he congratulated us on a job well done, and said to the captain of the SS Steel Director, nothing beats a good 'Blue Funnel man'.

Tuesday 23rd September we had an invite to a dinner from the Captain of the SS Steel Director, ashore in Bangkok. It was for the 2nd engineer, Paul, the chief, Tom and myself, and was a slap-up meal, with all that we could drink,' (dangerous)'. He also presented me with a large 'Spoon and Fork', made of hard wood from Bangkok, as a memento, (Still have them to this day). He also gave us 100US $.

Quite an eventful weekend...

*Some of my friends from the MV Anchises, yours truly is holding the fork.
2nd from the left is Chief Steward Jack Doyle*

Departure from Bangkok was 2230hrs on Wednesday, 24th September 1969. Next port of call Kota Kinabalu, in Sarawak,

Borneo. Weather hot,93degF, high humidity and no wind. Arrival at Kota Kinabalu, was in the early hours of the morning, 0130hrs., and we were tied up alongside by 0630hrs. Saturday, 27th September 1969.

Kota Kinabalu was a clean new city, the capital of the State of Sabah, like the places you see on films of the pacific islands. The jetty is only big enough for one ship, in a large crystal clear lagoon, lots of yacht's lie at anchor, near a huge posh looking hotel. Everything looks new, the lorries, cars, houses and buildings. The whole lagoon is surrounded by jungle and bushy hills and mountains, the peaks of which were hidden in cloud and mist, and probably many thousands of feet high. The name Kota Kinabalu means 'The city beneath the mountain'.

The Port of Kota Kinabalu, in September 1969. Also known as KK it is the capital of Malaysia's Sabah State in the Northern part of the island of Borneo. It is now a coastal city surrounded by a rainforest. Its known for its bustling markets its modern boardwalk, beaches and waterfront. It is also a gateway to The Kinabalu National Park and Mount Kinabalu.

On the Sunday we played another round of golf, a foursome, made up of the Captain, the Chief Engineer, the Chief Steward and myself, on the beautiful 8 hole course by the beach. What a beautiful setting with the palm trees and the waves rolling up to the edge of the immaculate greens. But even in the early morning it was very hot and the 9th tee was very welcome.

We sailed at 1730hrs for Sandakan.Arriving on the morning of the 30th September, loaded bags of coffee, sago and some timber and sailed again by 1700hrs the same day.

That did not however stop me from going ashore for a few hours to see what Sandakan had to offer. In those days, not a lot, a local people's market and a few roads of shops.

Our next port of call was Towau, at 0930hrs. Our anchorage was two miles off near a reef in a crystal clear lagoon. 350 tons of palm oil were loaded from a barge before leaving at 2030hrs and sailing for the small island of Bohiham.

This island's sole trade is timber and logs. Arrival there was 0530hrs on the 2nd October 1969, where we were greeted by the boss man, who lived on the only island house and he had about 100 men who came from many of the small islands, and loaded the ship with hardwood logs. His only entertainment was a film which was brought in by boat once every 5 months, and tonight was the night for the film.

The boss man works on the island for 3 months and has 3 days leave with relatives in Sandakan, then back to work again.

On the afternoon before we sailed, six young lads came to the ship in two dug-out canoes, asking for us to throw money over the side for them to dive down in the crystal clear water to retrieve it. They were very good at it …

By 1700hrs we were loaded and sailed for Sandakan, arriving at 0530hrs. Friday, 3rd October where we loaded another 350 tons of palm oil. It was raining heavily, and had cooled down a bit. The ship sailed at 1300hrs that day for Sibu, in the Rajang River in West Borneo.

Arrival was 1500hrs at anchor up the Rajang River on Sunday, 5th October 1969.

There were already two more ships at anchor, only one of them loading logs. A Ben Line boat and a new Russian ship. Cargo was worked. Logs were loaded into the holds after being floated to the side of the ship, with men walking the logs precariously, one by one.

Now these logs could weigh anything up to 15 tons and they were wet, so gave my winches a hard time, resulting in some breakdowns.

The other inconvenience up the jungle was the persistent mosquitoes, they were big and particularly nasty, not to mention the cockroaches.

On the Tuesday night we were invited over to a Russian ship for drinks, well, vodka.

The ship was an interesting vessel as it was, to the best of my knowledge, a Gas Turbine powered ship, and was very modern However, the Captain and 1st mate, who were both women,(although you would never know), would not divulge any information, about the ship, except that it was a Gas Turbine powered ship, and strangely had a sprinkler system over the mid ships accommodation.

It was possibly of the 'Leninsky Komosol class of merchant vessel, (probably the 'Parizhskaya Communa') built in the Kherson Shipyards in 1968. But what it was doing up the Rajang River, I cannot imagine, as to the best of knowledge it was not working cargo.

The following night we returned the invitation, and the whole ship practically, came over as I had offered to put on a film for them. They always liked the chance to see how the west lived, so I showed them the film 'From Russia with Love' a James Bond film.They absolutely loved it.

By Thursday 9th October 1969, at 1330hrs we were FSA from the Rajang river and headed for Singapore, due to arrive at 1830hrs on the 10th at 'Godown' 10 Singapore.

Ships in port were Phyrrus and the Centaur.

We had the weekend in Singapore, and knowing that this trip would in all probability be the last time that I would see Singapore, I spent considerable time ashore, photographing its people and its way of life. Cargo was worked most of the time, and our time of sailing was 1515hrs on Tuesday 14th October 1969, for Port Swettenham, where we would arrive by 0600hrs the following morning.

On the Friday the 17th October, the opportunity to travel up to Kuala Lumpur presented itself, so I caught the train to the city and was pleasantly surprised by the experience.

It was cheap, fast and efficient. The station in Kuala Lumpur, was all white and gold and immaculately clean, even though there were still oil fired steam engines as well as diesel trains in evidence. Naturally a trip to the local MPD (Motive Power Department) was organised, and even though it was very hot and humid it was well worth the effort. A trip into town showed that the people were happy and all seemed to have homes and jobs to go to, and it had the vibrancy of a modern city.

I returned to Port Swettenham on the modern diesel rail car service, which was full but on time and walked back to the ship via the seaman's mission, where I had a beer and later a hair cut.

Early Saturday morning the 18th October we sailed from Port Swettenham at 0630hrs for Trincomalee, Ceylon, ETA 1830hrs 21st October 1969.

We were still in the monsoon season, so anything could happen, but seas were only force 5-6, and choppy, and we were making a speed of some 16knots.

Arrival at Trincomalee was on schedule, and we tied up stern first to the jetty and 'lighters' appeared from all directions and our cargo of tea and more tea was loaded, until all our holds were full.

One always enjoyed Trincomalee, as it was so laid-back and a 'tomorrow will do' place.

To walk around after taking the water taxi from the ship,was always pleasant and safe, and full of photographic opportunities, and the people were always friendly.There was very little road traffic, and cars were usually old Morris Minors, usually black. How they kept them going, one would never know. There were oxen carts and bicycles, cows and animals everywhere, and the smells, especially from the fish markets, were something that has to be experienced. On the beaches were fishermen, with their hollowed out canoes, with outriggers that were lashed on and with huge white sails, mending their nets. There were children playing, and women selling their wares.

The oxen cart, a common form of transport on Sri Lanka
(or as it was in 1969 Ceylon)

A game of football was usually organised by the agents. This time we played against the young lads of St Josephs'. We never won as they were much fitter than us and used to the heat, but a 6-2 defeat was quite reasonable, and we all enjoyed the experience.

We sailed for Columbo, in North Ceylon on Monday 27th October 1969 at 0800hrs. Our ETA was 0600hrs 28th October.

Another common form of transport was the shoulder yoke

Colombo in Ceylon always was a busy port with ships from all over the world.
The SS Myrmidon originally a 'Victory' boat built in the USA in 1945,
by Permanente Metals, in Richmond California. and purchased as one
of six by Alfred Holt to replace war losses, originally called Ripon Victory
gave A/H service until about 1971, when she was laid up along with other
Victory boats in the River Fal, and was subsequently broken up in
Kaohsiung later that year

It was still the monsoon season, but we were lucky and had a relatively steady passage to Colombo and would only be staying for two days. This would include 'full bunkers' and water ready for the long crossing of the Indian ocean to Capetown.

We tied up at the buoys in the harbour at 0800hrs, Tuesday 28th October 1969, waiting to go alongside.

We eventually tied up alongside, for cargo and bunkers, but were informed that there was a 24 hours strike, which delayed us on our scheduled departure.

However, this gave me the opportunity to go ashore to stretch my legs before the long voyage south, across the Indian Ocean to Capetown.

We sailed from Colombo at 0900hrs on the 30th October 1969, into the pure blue of the Indian Ocean. We were FSA by 1000hrs. It was wind force 2/3 calm and warm.

The good weather lasted for most of the voyage to Capetown, and the days were taken up with ship's maintenance schedules and voyage reports.

We called in at Capetown for the mail and to send off our voyage reports, and said our goodbyes to Table Mountain, for what I thought would be the last time, but as time would tell, that was not to be., but then that would be the subject of another story.

Now with a following wind and albatrosses for company, it would be 12 days before we were due in Las Palmas, on the 22nd November 1969.

We were, however, running short of boiler oil, so would have to take on fuel at Las Palmas.

This was organised through the agents, but did delay our schedule for some hours.

Now as any seafarer will tell you some ships are happy ships and some are not... Very often this is caused not just by the weather or the schedule, but by the quality of the food on board.

The Anchises, on this trip was not a particularly happy ship as the chief stewards food left a lot to be desired, so this would cause many of us to be more than glad to be back in port, where one couldn't wait to get a tasty meal ashore.

With a day to go before Las Palmas we saw a number of ships heading South down the Atlantic.

A ship of the Clan Line at sea

A Moore Mc Cormack Lines ship with derricks aloft ready for loading and unloading cargo

Fuel oil was taken on at Las Palmas, just sufficient to get us to London, and our departure was 0600hrs Sunday 23rd November 1969. It wasn't very long before we had to change into 'Blues' as the weather deteriorated and it got colder and colder and as per norm the Bay of Biscay had its customary long swells. This was also accompanied by a force 11 gale, which continued until we reached the Brixham pilot, on the 27th November. The gale subsided by the time we reached the Gravesend pilot at 0200hrs on the 28th November, and we were alongside in Surrey Commercial dock by 0630hrs.

The ship was cleared for customs and immigration and my 'relief' arrived at 1200hrs. The handover was given and I said my goodbyes and was on the 1600hrs train from Euston to Manchester.

There were then 7 weeks leave outstanding, and I had already worked more than my three months statutory notice, therefore releasing me from my contract. Then with P60 in hand was free to move on to a shore-side job.

Whether or not that was the right move only time would tell…

7

Vivid Memories from my Days at Sea

A foggy day in the Channel – all shipping is running at slow ahead and the fog horns wail sometimes every thirty seconds, both from the ships and the land. A long low sound... Gravesend, Brixham, The Needles-unforgettable. I can hear it now now now...

The sounds of the sea, the lapping of the waves on the bow, the rushing of the waves down the sides, the roar and turbulence of the stern propellers, and the wake that disappears into the distance...

The vibration, distant throb of the engines, as you lay in your bunk, rocks you to sleep. You learn to read what the weather is like by that vibration. If the vibration suddenly changes you know that there could be a problem, or standby is imminent. It becomes your sixth sense.

'Sea legs'. After a few days you adapt to the ship's movement, and when you go ashore, after a considerable voyage, it takes a while to compensate.

When travelling from West to East you lose time, and when travelling from East to West you gain time. Your body has to quickly learn to compensate.

Albatrosses, dolphins, porpoises and whales – all friends of the sea.

Sometimes they can accompany the ship for many days. The albatross always seems to be looking at you. Sometimes she flies at deck height, sometimes at bridge deck height With its wing tips almost within touching distance, this huge bird stays on the wing for days, and can be three to four meters wide tip to tip.

An Albatross follows us at sea. They range the Southern oceans and can have a wingspan in excess of 3 metres and live for over 40 years.

Sitting on the bows and watching the dolphins and porpoises, ride the bow wave can be mesmerising I used to spend hours watching them.

Waking up in the morning to find a deck full of flying fish, that had landed and were stranded. Life was full of new experiences.

Arriving in a channel, or approach to a port or river and the sight of a pilot boat greets you. You are mesmerised by the tiny dot that gets bigger and eventually comes alongside to off load the pilot, who deftly climbs up either a ships ladder or a moving gangplank, he then manoeuvres the ship safely into port. The same in reverse to get the ship back out to sea.

Pilot boats, come in all shapes and sizes, from the vary old to the very new.

Tugs would assist the ships to dock safely, seen in most ports in the days when there were no 'bow thrusters' or 'Stern thrusters'.

Tug boats. All 'Rea' Tugs in the 1960's ended in '-garth'. This example was Cedergarth, a diesel tug. She was built by P K Harris shipyards at Appledore in 1962, and weighed in at 213tons.

Rea tug – Rosegarth. Built in the yards of Alexander Hall & Co in Aberdeen in 1954. She was a triple expansion steam-engine tug, and spent most of her life in Liverpool before being sold on in 1970 and subsequently broken up in 1984, in Messina

Sights that stick in your mind, a sea of cranes, slipways and steel like the John Brown's shipyards of the Clyde...

When Britain was Great ... The QE2 being fitted out at John Browns shipyards on the River Clyde... in 1967. She was a Steam Turbine driven ship, (2 Turbines) and was 58,000 tons. With a service speed of 28.5 knots and a maximum speed of 34knots she was a fast cruise liner for the day.

Like the lines of ships along the docksides in Singapore, busy busy busy.

Or closer to home, Birkenhead. The MV Prometheus Built by Vickers Armstrong's of Newcastle on Tyne in 1967, and after many years of service she was broken up in Kaohsiung in 1986

When first arriving in port in the Far East, and ordering a bag of prawn crackers.

The smell of the foliage, the hustle and bustle of the myriad of small craft, the noise of the docks, which goes on 24hrs, going ashore, having that first ice cold beer with friends, walking ashore, taking in the ambience, the people, the sights, sounds and smells, going for a meal, one that you have never experienced before, what to eat, what not to eat-that is always the question.

The mail from home arrives, from the agents. The excitement and anticipation of what news it may contain, good or bad or otherwise...

Listening to a steel band playing on the Jamaican ship next to you, off the aft end of your ship.

Fishing, with the Chinese crew also off the aft end, for small shark, and enjoying sharks fin soup, cooked by them.

8

Phenomena at Sea

The Doldrums, when the sea is becalmed and literally looks like a millpond, which can be for days, can produce fogbanks, can be very oppressive, hot and humid. The doldrums can be from 5 degrees North of the equator to 5 degrees South of the equator.

What are the Doldrums. The **doldrums** is a colloquial expression derived from historical maritime usage, which refers to those parts of the Atlantic Ocean and the Pacific Ocean affected by the Inter tropical Convergence Zone, a low-pressure area around the equator where the prevailing winds are calm.

The colour of the sea around the UK is mostly a grey colour. As you journey South into warmer climates it seems to turn blue and in places like the Malacca Straits, near Singapore, it seems to turn green with phosphorescent waves.

A Hurricane. Sailing through the eye is quite dynamic. Depending on how big the hurricane spiral is it can take hours before the turmoil of the wind abates and the still of the eye is witnessed, and hours again going out the other side.

Whirlpools... Stay away from them as many a ship has disappeared without trace-a very powerful vortex that draws you in and sucks you down.,down.,down.

The beautiful animals of the sea:- the whales, the dolphins, the porpoises, and the fish.
The coral reefs and islands, and crystal clear lagoons and waters.

The ports, the straits and the roads of the sea, the sand-banks and the rocks.

The deltas, the rivers and the lakes and the canals.

The locks and docks, the wharfs and quays and the steps, all form part of the maritime scene.

The sea has many moods, from a long slow swell to a violently rough gale force wind- driven wave, and occasionally a rogue wave, that can do untold damage and in some cases completely wreck or sink a ship. Then there is the ultimate wave, a Tsunami wave, the most destructive, to be avoided whenever possible.

On Board ship.

The tank cleaners. These were the men and women who cleaned out the deep tanks prior to loading palm oil or latex. They used their own lighting and it was invariably dodgy. They always asked for the 'lece' (the electrician), for the best place to plug it in. You could guarantee it would trip the breakers at some point in the operation. The Bamboo scaffolding was always dodgy and 'Harry Clough'. How they ever got the job done I will never know, but they did, and always singing as they did it (They must have been high on something). If I remember correctly they brought their own cooks and pots and pans and the whole 'toot'...

Engine room procedures... The electrician's main job, on stand-by, was to man the switch board, and maintain power supply to the most important places, and shed load if necessary.

What is 'standby'?? It is that time when the ship is manoeuvring in and out of port, or any time that the ship is not FSA (Full Speed Away) or stopped waiting for further action, or for receiving instructions from the bridge.

The electrician can be expected to take control of the 'sticks' (Main Engine Controls), answer telegraphs, signals from the bridge and to write down all movements in the log book – sometimes all of that at the same time. If you miss a movement it can not only be dangerous for the ship, but costly in the bar that evening- meaning the beers are 'on you'.

Steering gear procedures... These are very dependent on the types of ship, A/H ships had several backup systems for the steering gear.

The main system was two telemotors forcing two hydraulic rams back and forth. This can also be done by a steering wheel off the aft end of the ship, if the power fails by batteries, and by two chain blocks. Once per trip it is usually tested.

Lowering of the boats, for 'boat drill'. This was part of the electricians job, he had to bring and clamp on the portable electric motors for the lowering of the boats from their 'davits'.

These motors were an important maintenance item during the voyage.

The other important part of the job for the electrician was the maintenance of the winches used in cargo handling. There were usually four winches and four derricks per hatch and these would be systematically overhauled each trip. The fewer break downs the better.

All other electrical equipment would be on a planned maintenance schedule for the voyage and would be systematically worked through each voyage.

One couldn't forget Mary the 'Sew Sew' lady, who would come on board and do all those sewing jobs that you didn't or couldn't do.

And of course one must never forget the stewards and the cooks and the cabin boys, who helped make your trip that bit more comfortable, and to Alfred Holts for some of the greatest ships that I was ever been privileged to sail aboard and to get paid for doing just that...

Phil Braithwaite R848947...

The MV Diomed, Built in 1956 by The Caledon Shipbuilding Co of Dundee.
She was a training ship for Midshipmen and was also used to give personnel
from India Buildings the opportunity to witness the Far East at first hand.
She was later renamed The Glenbeg. She was later sold on and again renamed
as the Kaising, which she kept until scrapped in 1982 in Kaohsiung.

"I would like to dedicate this book
to the memory of Alfred Holt and company,
founder of that big Blue Funnel.
(1829 to 1911)."